A Treatise on Skating
Revisited and Enhanced

A Treatise on Skating

Revisited and Enhanced

By Robert Jones

With contributions by W. E. Cormack

Edited by B. A. Thurber

Skating History Press

Main text originally published in 1772.
Additional material published in 1780, 1782, 1797, 1823, and 1855.
Explanatory material © 2017, 2023 B. A. Thurber.
All rights reserved.
Cover image: The Fencing Position (1772). Collection Niko Mulder.

ISBN: 978-1-948100-10-6
LCCN: 2023923353

Skating History Press
Evanston, IL
http://www.skatinghistorypress.com/

Contents

Preface ix

Introduction 1

Skating in Great Britain 3

Robert Jones and his treatise 11

Content and reception 19

Editorial process 25

A Treatise on Skating 27

Dedication 31

Preface 33

Section I 37
    Of the different methods of fixing on skates . . 37
    Of the construction of skates 40
    Of the first position 45
    Of the inside edge 48
    Of travelling on the inside edge 49
    Of the outside edge 54
    Of travelling on the outside edge 56

Of the curved line on the outside edge, called rolling	57
Of running	59

Section II   65

Of the spiral line	65
Of the inside circle	66
Of the outside circle	68
Of the flying Mercury	69
Of the fencing position	69
Of the salutation	73
Of the serpentine line	77
Of travelling backwards	78
To cut the figure of a heart on one leg	78

Later Additions   81

The Skater's March   83

The editor to the reader   88

Preface to the 1823 edition   93

Revised 1823 preface   99

Preface to the 1855 edition   105

New and revised instructions   107

Of the construction of skates, and the different methods of fixing them to the foot	107
Travelling backwards	113
Outside wheel and outside edge backwards	114

Serpentine line backwards 115
Concluding injunction 115

Commentary 119

Notes 121

Editions of the *Treatise* 135
Under the original title 137
    1772 137
    1775? 139
    1780? 140
    1797 142
    1818 142
Under the revised title 143
    1823 143
    1825 144
    1855 145
    1865 146
Recent 147
    2017 147
    2023 147

Robert Jones's skates 149
London and Edinburgh 149
Blade curvature 155

Bibliography 163

List of Figures

1	A caricature of Jones?	13
2	Six of the most approved methods of appearing ridiculous on the ice!!	21
3	Two views of an English skate (1772).	44
4	A journey on a road six feet broad (1772).	51
5	A journey on a road eight feet broad (1772).	52
6	Common rolling (1772).	60
7	Rolling (1823).	61
8	Common rolling (1855).	62
9	The inside circle (1855).	67
10	The flying Mercury (1772).	70
11	The Mercury position (1823).	71
12	The flying Mercury (1855).	72
13	The fencing position (1772).	74
14	The fencing position (1823).	75
15	The fencing position (1855).	76
16	Announcement of a performance that included the Skater's March at the Theatre Royal in Edinburgh.	89
17	The outside wheel and outside edge backwards (1855).	116
C1	Drawing of a bone skate found at Moorfields, London.	121
C2	The most popular type of skate described by Vandervell and Witham (1869).	131
C3	A skate with a cramp.	132
C4	Rodgers' patent skate	134

C5	Cold Broth and Calamity by Thomas Rowlandson (1792).	151
C6	William Grant's skates (1782).	152
C7	Robert Walker's left foot (1790s).	153
C8	The blade as part of a circle.	156
C9	The triangle to use for calculating the rocker radius.	157
C10	Robert Jones's skates reconstructed.	160

List of Tables

1   Availability of the various editions. . . . 136

Preface

A lot has happened since the 2017 edition of this book. More materials have become available online. This gave me some new things to add and helped me solve some of the problems I noted then.

Bev Thurber
December, 2023

Introduction

Skating in Great Britain

The publication of Robert Jones's *Treatise on Skating* in 1772 marks a new era in skating history. It was the first (or if not the first, the oldest known today) manual of skating technique. But it does not mark the beginning of skating in Great Britain; instead, it follows a long tradition of people of all classes skating for fun.

Jones begins his book with bone skates, and I may as well begin there too. People began skating in England no later than the tenth century, when Scandinavian settlers glided across ice on skates made from the leg bones of animals. Skaters stood on smoothed bones (attaching them to their feet was optional) and pushed themselves along with poles. Jones clearly knew about this, because he begins his *Treatise* with a quote from William FitzStephen's twelfth-century *Description of London* (page 33), which is the oldest extant description of skating in England. He may not have known that bone skates were still used in England during his time and into the nineteenth century.* Arthur Mac-

---

*Three references to bone skates in use in England during the late nineteenth century are collected in B. A. Thurber, *Skates Made of Bone: A History* (Jefferson, NC: McFarland, 2020), 141.

Gregor has summarized the archaeological evidence for bone skates in Great Britain,[*] and I have argued that they brought there by Scandinavian settlers.[†]

While fun to use, bone skates had certain limitations. It was extremely difficult to stop or turn on them, as P. A. Säve vividly described:

> ...when sliding, you cannot turn aside or change course if you see a deep hole in front of you. The only thing to do in this case is to set the pole between the legs, lean back on it, and let it scratch the ice to slightly arrest the motion...[‡]

This problem was not resolved until metal-bladed skates were invented. The earliest ones looked like blocks of wood wrapped in metal bars nearly a centimeter wide. They made their first appearance in the archaeological record in the early thirteenth century in the Netherlands[§] and were probably quite expensive,[¶] which meant skating on them was restricted to the wealthy.

---

[*] Arthur MacGregor, "Bone skates: A review of the evidence," *Archaeological Journal* 133 (1976): 57–74.

[†] Thurber, *Skates Made of Bone*, 107–114.

[‡] P. A. Säve and H. Gustavson, *Gotländska lekar*, vol. 1, Svenska lekar (Uppsala: Almqvist och Wichsells Boktryckeri AB, 1948), 77.

[§] Wiebe Blauw, *Van glis tot klapschaats: Schaatsen en schaatsenmakers in Nederland, 1200 tot heden* (Franeker: Van Wijnen, 2001), 57.

[¶] Niko Mulder, "Ten IJse (1)," *Kouwe Drukte* 12, no. 33 (October 2008): 26.

It is not clear when metal-bladed skates arrived in Great Britain. I've heard several different stories, none with enough evidence to bear retelling. The first clear evidence for skating in England appeared in 1662. Two diarists, John Evelyn and Samuel Pepys, observed skaters on December 1, 1662.* Evelyn described

> the strange, and wonderfull dexterity of the sliders on the new Canall in St. James's park, perform'd by divers Gent: & others with Scheets, after the manner of the Hollanders, with what pernicitie & swiftnesse they passe, how sudainly they stop in full carriere upon the Ice, before their Majesties.†

Pepys called skating "a very pretty art"‡ and followed up with two additional mentions, on the eighth and the fifteenth of the same year.§

These sightings opened a veritable flood of English-language skating materials. Under "Blade Skating," Foster¶ listed eight mentions of skating in books published in England (or elsewhere but in English) between the diarists and Jones's book:

---

*Foster (*A Bibliography of Skating*) remarks, "I have found no earlier evidence of Blade Skating in England than these references of Evelyn and Pepys."

†E. S. de Beer, ed., *The Diary of John Evelyn* (Oxford: Oxford University Press, 1959), 448–449.

‡Mynors Bright, ed., *Diary and Correspondence of Samuel Pepys, Esp., F.R.S.: From His MS. Cypher in the Pepysian Library* (New York: Dodd, Mead, 1904), 41.

§Bright, 45, 48–49.

¶Foster, *A Bibliography of Skating*, 26–30.

1671: Stephen Skinner included an entry for "Scates" in his *Etymologicon linguæ Anglicanæ.*

1683/4: Skating at the Frost Fair on the River Thames was commemorated in a number of ballads collected by Edward F. Rimbault.*

1688: William Carr[†] described how "the nimble Dutchmen on their scatses, so long as the ice would bear them, did shoot down the French"; Foster notes that this is "false history"—those "scatses" were really crampons.[‡]

1699: Philip Frowde included a 58-line Latin poem on skating, "Cursus glacialis, Anglicè Scating," in volume 2 of his *Musarum Anglicanarum Analecta.*

1711: On January 31, Jonathan Swift wrote a letter to Esther Johnson in which he remarked, "The canal and Rosamond's Pond [are] full of rabble, sliding, and with skates, if you know what those are?"[§]

1720: Edmund Curll published an English translation of Frowde's poem under the title *Scating: A Poem.*

---

*Edward F. Rimbault, *Old Ballads Illustrating the Great Frost of 1683–4 and the Fair on the River Thames* (London: T. Richards for the Percy Society, 1844).

[†]William Carr, *Remarks of the Government of severall parts of Germanie, Denmark, Sweedland, Hamburg, Lubeck, and Hansiatique townes, but more particularly of the United Provinces* (Amsterdam: n.p., 1688).

[‡]Quoted (with comments) in Foster, *A Bibliography of Skating*, 27.

[§]Quoted in Foster, 28.

1730: James Thomson's *Winter: A Poem* (1726) includes several mentions of skating—but not until 1730, when the poems for all four seasons were assembled in one volume. The textual history of the poem is described well in Otto Zippel's dissertation[*] and critical edition.[†]

1754: Count D'Avaux, the French ambassador to the Netherlands, saw the Princess of Orange skating and wrote about it in a book translated into English in 1754 and 1755. Foster,[‡] like many more recent skating historians, only includes the sentence about how extraordinary the sight was; the full passage from the entry for January 25, 1685, is reproduced here:

> It looked also as if the Prince of Orange's temper was altered, or that he had some impenetrable design, for he, who is so jealous that he does not permit his Princess to receive any private visit, not only from men, but women, presses the Duke of Monmouth to go after dinner to her, to teach her country-dances. They even made her act in characters which are unsuitable to a Princess, and which I should term ridiculous

---

[*]Otto Zippel, "Entstehungs- und Entwicklungsgeschichte von Thomsons «Winter»" (PhD diss., Friedrich-Wilhelms-Universität zu Berlin, 1907).

[†]Otto Zippel, *Thomson's Seasons: Critical Edition* (Berlin: Mayer & Müller, 1908).

[‡]Foster, *A Bibliography of Skating*, 20.

in an ordinary woman: for, in the great frost, which happened this year [1685], the Prince of Orange obliged her (such is her complaisance to him) to learn to skate upon the ice, because the Duke of Monmouth was also desirous of learning it. Twas a very extraordinary thing to see the Princess of Orange, with very short petticoats, and those tucked up half way to her waist, and with iron pattins on her feet, learning to slide, sometimes on one foot, sometimes on the other.*

A few more items can be added to this list. In 1763, *British Magazine* reported a skating race in the fens:

Feb. 4th, 1763. A few days ago Mr. John Lamb and Mr. George Fawn, of Wisbeach, ran a skaiting match from hence to Whittlesea for ten guineas a side, which was won by Mr. Lamb, who skaited it in 46 minutes, being 15 measured miles.[†]

---

*Comte d'Avaux, *The Negotiations of Count d'Avaux* (London: A. Millar, D. Wilson, & T. Durham, 1754–1755), III.132.

[†]Quoted in "Historical Catalogue of the Exhibition of Skates, with Pictures and Other Matters Relating to Skating and Skaters, Held at the Hall of the Alpine Club, Feb. 10th to Feb. 15th, 1902," in *A History of the National Skating Association of Great Britain, 1879–1901* (London: National Skating Association, 1902), 71.

This was called "the oldest record of a British race till now traced" in the catalogue of the 1902 NSA exhibiton,* which included it under "errata and addenda." Foster couldn't have included it in his *Bibliography* a few years earlier because he didn't know about it.

Foster included two other important works under "Skee Running," which is precisely where they belong.[†] These were Thomas Percy's 1763 and 1700 translations of Old Norse texts.[‡] Percy saw skating where it wasn't and envisioned King Harold on skates (instead of skis) and Thialfi competing in a skating race on a snowy plain (instead of a footrace on level ground).[§] In Percy's defense, the latter error actually came from Paul Henri Mallet's French translation of the *Prose Edda* and also made its way into Friedrich Gottlieb Klopstock's poetry: *Die Kunst Tialfs* (Thialf's Art, 1767) appears to be based on this mistake.[¶]

In addition, Britain's first formal skating club, the Edinburgh Skating Club, was probably founded in the 1740s. Richard Stephenson puts the most likely date at about 1744 based on research conducted on a visit

---

*"Historical Catalogue of the Exhibition of Skates," 71.

[†]Foster, *A Bibliography of Skating*, 6.

[‡]Thomas Percy, trans., *Five Pieces of Runic Poetry, Translated from the Islandic Language* (London: R. and J. Dodsley, 1763); Paul Henri Mallet, *Northern Antiquities: Or a Description of the Manners, Customs, Religion and Laws of the Ancient Danes, Including Those of Our Own Saxon Ancestors*, trans. Thomas Percy (London: T. Carnan, 1770).

[§]Thurber, *Skates Made of Bone*, 40–41.

[¶]Foster, *A Bibliography of Skating*, 29.

to Edinburgh.* By 1772, skating had become popular enough that the market was ready for a book on how to do it.

---

*Richard Stephenson, "In the Beginning," *Skating*, June 1970, 8–9.

Robert Jones and his treatise

Robert Jones was born in about 1740,* possibly in North Wales,† but his father was, according to one report, a tailor in London. A "remarkably witty and clever" man, Robert Jones was remembered for inventing "nocturnal watches to tell the hour in the darkest night" and appears to have been a fixture in London society, where he famously dressed up as Punch for a party.‡ Jones has gone down in history for three main achievements: his book about fireworks, his book about skating, and his conviction for sodomizing a young boy—in that order.

Jones's first book, *A New Treatise on Artificial Fireworks* (1765) provides instructions for making fireworks of various types. As a boy, Jones was "particularly active and clever in making fire-works."§ He was recruited to the military by one Mr. Pitt (Lord Chatham) and

---

*According to Alexander Hope's testimony at his trial in 1772, he was 15 or 16 years old 17 years earlier (see Rictor Norton, ed., "The trial of Robert Jones, 1772," in *Homosexuality in Eighteenth-Century England: A Sourcebook* (2004)). That puts his age in 1772 at 31 or 32 and his birth in about 1740.

†Jones's origin was reported by the *Oxford Journal* in July 1772, as quoted by Rictor Norton, "The first public debate about homosexuality in England: News reports concerning the case of Captain Jones, 1772," in *Homosexuality in Eighteenth-Century England: A Sourcebook* (2004; updated 8 August 2022.).

‡According to an anonymous correspondent of the *Gazetteer and New Daily Advertiser* in a letter published July 25, 1772, and collected in Norton.

§According to the anonymous correspondent.

"raised himself by his merit" to the rank of lieutenant in the Royal artillery force by 1772.* Though many documents from this period refer to him as captain, lieutenant was his correct rank.

Jones's *Treatise on Skating* first appears in list of new books in the February 1772 edition (but not the January 1772 edition) of the *Critical Review*'s "Monthly Catalogue."† This means it was published—or at least available for order—early in the year, during skating season, when it would have been most useful. The *Critical Review* says:

> To behold an engineer practising his manoeuvres on the glacis, would not be an extraordinary occurrence, but this impetuous gentleman, whose excursions even the ramparts cannot restrain, has fairly led us upon the ice. The temperature of the air at present will not admit of our reducing this author's rule to practice, we shall therefore only observe, that no critic ever delivered more excellent injunctions for the management of either the buskin or soc, than Mr. Jones does for that of the skates.

According to the *Gazetteer and New Daily Advertiser*'s anonymous correspondent, Jones "bore an irre-

---

*Rictor Norton, "Jones, Captain Robert," in *Who's Who in Gay and Lesbian History: From Antiquity to World War II*, second ed., ed. Robert Aldrich and Gary Wotherspoon (New York: Routledge, 2002), 275.

†"Monthly catalogue," *The Critical Review: Or, Annals of Literature* 33 (1772): #54, p. 184.

Figure 1: A caricature of Jones?

proachable character" and "supported his mother and sister"—until the summer after his skating book was published. In July 1772, after a public trial, Jones was convicted of sodomizing Francis Henry Hay, who was then $12\frac{1}{2}$ years old.* Rictor Norton has assembled numerous materials pertaining to the trial, including all the testimony and many newspaper articles, on his website.[†]

Jones was sentenced to death in July, 1772, and Hines[‡] reports that he died that same year, but the further reports collected by Norton tell a different story. His execution was scheduled for August 5, 1772. Just one day before that, the *Manchester Mercury* reported

> It is thought that Capt. Jones, who is now under Sentence of Death for an unnatural Crime, will received his Majesty's most gracious Pardon; as some Gentlemen of the first Rank and fortune in the County of Suffolk, as well as the celebrated Mr. Dryb—r [i.e. Drybutter], and the whole Maccaroni Club, intend to convince a Great Personage

---

*Hay's age is often given as 13, but the trial ends with a statement that he would turn 13 on January 31, 1773, making him 12 during the trial. See Norton, "The trial of Robert Jones, 1772."

[†]Rictor Norton, "The first public debate about homosexuality in England: The Case of Captain Jones, 1772," in *The Gay Subculture in Georgian England* (2004; updated 10 May 2014.).

[‡]James R. Hines, *Figure Skating: A History* (Urbana: University of Illinois Press, 2006), 27n5.

[i.e. the King], that a Man or [sic] Taste should not lose his Life, for the Amore pio Pueri.*

Indeed, at noon, "a warrant was sent from the office of one of his Majesty's Secretaries of State, ordering a respite of the execution of Robert Jones until Tuesday the 11th instant."†

Jones had six more days to live. During that time, his friends and colleagues petitioned the Duke of Gloucester and the King to pardon him. On August 10, his execution was stayed for another week or "until his Majesty's pleasure shall be further signified," depending on the paper.‡ From August 20, papers reported that Jones would be pardoned by the King around the end of the month. The *General Evening Post*, *Aris's Birmingham Gazette*, and the *Stamford Mercury* reported that he would go to America. A few days later, the *General Evening Post* added that he would

> not be received into the East-India service, not withstanding what has been said to the contrary; and it is a reflection upon the gen-

---

*All newspaper coverage of Jones's trial and its aftermath is quoted in Norton, "The first public debate about homosexuality in England: News reports concerning the case of Captain Jones, 1772."

†*Gazetteer and New Daily Advertiser*, August 5, 1772.

‡Several papers reported the one-week stay; *The Craftsman, or Say's Weekly Journal* reported the possibility of a longer one on August 15, 1772.

tlemen in it to think that they will rank with any man who has been dismissed with infamy from his Majesty's.*

The pardon came through by September 7 on the condition that he leave the country within a month and never return. It took a bit longer; Jones wasn't released from prison until the end of October. But he did go, and was allegedly living "in grandeur with a lovely Ganymede (his footboy) at Lyons, in the South of France" by June, 1773.†

On April 21, 1777, the *Morning Post* reported that Jones was a commander in the Persian Army. On April 14, 1785, the *Hereford Journal* claimed that "however extraordinary it may appear, [Jones] is at present Mustapha General to the Bombardiers in the service of the Grand Signor." According to the *Times*, Jones had a reputation as "an excellent artillerist and engineer—to him it is that the Turks are indebted for the skill which they have shewn in the management of their guns, and in the defence of their fortified places."‡ A few months later, the *Times* added that he was

> in the service of one of [several Beys]...at the time of their rebellion against the Sublime Porte, and reported to have been put to death, with near 30,000 others of the vanquished party.§

---

*August 27–29, 1772.
†Cutting from an unknown source.
‡Issue 1096, June 12, 1788.
§Issue 1190, December 6, 1788.

If this is correct, Jones lived in exile for 16 years after his conviction.

Content and reception

Jones's *Treatise on Skating* was primarily aimed at beginning skaters. It claims not to cover all the skating movements of his time, only the ones that were "graceful" and "pleasing" (page 79). After explaining the basics, the book emphasizes looking good on the ice. Jones's express goal was to promote "easy movement and graceful attitude" (page 41).

Section I helps new skaters get started. It covers the basics: choosing skates, putting them on, and skating on forward outside and inside edges. Section II covers "the more masterly parts of this art" (page 65) and focuses on body positions, including the flying Mercury and the fencing position. Jones calls these moves "figures," but the context makes it clear that this refers to body positions rather than the marks on the ice that were eventually codified into the set of compulsory figures that formed the basis of figure skating. This emphasis on posture and appearance makes skating as described by Jones similar to modern free skating. Jones's only clear reference the tracings skates leave on the ice comes at the very end of the book: Jones's "figure of a heart on one leg" (page 78) is clearly a figure drawn on the ice.

All of this was packed into a relatively small number of pages. The first edition was only 64 pages or approximately 10,000 words long and included plates engraved by William Darling. The book's influence is highlighted by a 1796 engraving by Isaac Cruikshank called "Six of the most approved methods of appearing ridiculous on the ice!!" that shows several of Jones's moves (figure 2). The accompanying text reads

> The *Serpentine River* in the winter season affords an appearance highly diverting; Lords and Commoners repair to the ice, which cracks and bends incessantly beneath its motley load, while on every side, *gin* and *gingerbread* are liberally distributed for *ready money only*, the salubrity of which instantly dispels the effects of *cold, falls,* and *contusions.*
>
> *Scating* when well executed is pleasing to the spectator and performer, but where the attempt is made by a *fat* unwieldy man, writhing his body into a variety of postures, and unsuccessful efforts at agility, the effect is truly ridiculous; this I have endeavoured to represent in Plate IX [figure 2], displaying six of the *most approv'd* methods of *appearing ridiculous on the ice!*[*]

At least three more editions were produced in the eighteenth century.[†] The *Treatise* was revived with a reprint in 1818 and a new edition with the title *The*

---

[*]G. M. Woodward, *Eccentric Excursions: or, Literary and Pictorial Sketches of Countenance, Character and Country in different parts of England and South Wales* (London: Allen & Co., 1796), 22.

[†]All the editions are summarized starting on page 135. The first five (1772–1818) were published under the original title and included the original plates.

Figure 2: Six of the most approved methods of appearing ridiculous on the ice!! From G. M. Woodward, *Eccentric Excursions: or, Literary and Pictorial Sketches of Countenance, Character and Country in different parts of England and South Wales* (London: Allen & Co., 1796).

Art of Skating Practically Explained in 1823. This version included new pictures, a revised preface, and other small changes. The title page of this version restored Jones's proper rank (Lieutenant, not Captain) and claimed it was "printed for the author", which Nigel Brown[*] took as evidence that Jones still lived. If so, he would have been about 83 years old. This conflicts with the *Times*'s report of his death in 1788 (page 16).

Perhaps "the author" was whoever was responsible for the revisions—possibly William Eppes (or Epps) Cormack (5 May 1796–30 April 1868), whose name was added to the title page of the 1855 edition to give him credit for revising and adding to the text. Cormack had spent much of his life in Canada, with a brief break to study in Scotland. He is best known for his detailed description of Newfoundland, which was based on his explorations.[†] Skating was a hobby of his, and he was still spending time on the ice when he was 70 years old.[‡]

According to the preface to the 1855 edition (page 105), there were "loud calls" for a new version of Jones's book in 1852. The reason for these calls was not specified, but perhaps not coincidentally, 1852 is the year in which the first edition of *The Art of Skating* by John Cyclos (George Anderson) was published. This was "the only work at all worthy of the art," according to

---

[*]Nigel Brown, "Skating: 'a very pretty art'," *The Book Collector* 25, no. 6 (1977): 545.

[†]W. E. Cormack, *Narrative of a Journey across the Island of Newfoundland in 1822* (St. John's, Newfoundland?: (n.p.), 1856).

[‡]G. M. Story, "Cormack, William Eppes (Epps)," in *Dictionary of Canadian Biography*, vol. 9 (Toronto: University of Toronto, 2003).

Vandervell and Witham,* and was translated into German and Swedish in the next few years. Cyclos called Jones's book "good enough...but not sufficiently complete to supersede the want of a more comprehensive work" and add that it was

> erroneous in many respects, and deficient in others. The backward circles seem not to have been known then, for only in his last paragraph does he hint at such a possibility, where he mentions, as "newly discovered," the "heart-shaped" figure, corresponding to our figure **3**. Moreover, the book was written in the days of cocked hats and minuets, when every act of life was a sample of cold, studied, and acted formality, and it is therefore too punctilious about attitudes to suit the ideas of the present day. For the illustrations, the Author is indebted to this old work, and he adopted them because the ancient costume seemed better suited for the representation.[†]

Despite his criticism, Cyclos clearly leaned heavily

---

*H. E. Vandervell and T. Maxwell Witham, *A System of Figure-Skating, Being the Theory and Practice of the Art as Developed in England, with a Glance at Its Origin and History* (London: Macmillan & Company, 1869), vi.

†John Cyclos, *The Art of Skating with Plain Directions for the Acquirement of the Most Difficult and Elegant Maneuvers* (Glasgow: Thomas Murray & Son, 1852), v–vi.

on Jones's work. He reproduced Jones's figures with the heading "Skating, as in the Olden Time." When he quoted Jones, he felt free to disagree:

> Captain Jones thinks that a very firm fastening leaves the skate "no proper play," and considers that a fault; but I do not know what he seeks play in the skate for. I think the more it can be united with the foot the better.*

Such criticism may have provided the impetus for a revised version of Jones's book. Cormack's version included updated illustrations featuring skaters in then-current fashions and an expanded repertoire of figures. It was reprinted in 1865 with a few minor changes, mainly to punctuation and capitalization. Its publication then lapsed until the current century, when various editions were scanned for Gale Eighteenth-Century Collections Online (ECCO) and Google Books, and the former made printed and bound copies of its scanned versions available.

---

*Cyclos, *The Art of Skating with Plain Directions for the Acquirement of the Most Difficult and Elegant Maneuvers*, 35.

Editorial process

The present edition represents the second new edition of the book since 1865. It is a substantial revision of the 2017 edition. The main text is based on the 1772 edition. My additions are in square brackets [for figure numbers] and endnotes. I have left the occasionally idiosyncratic spelling, punctuation, and capitalization alone, except for standardizing the capitalization of the section headings. This means that some spellings are odd, like "jirks" for "jerks" (page 38). I accepted the errata unless otherwise noted. For consistency, I changed "skait" to "skate" throughout the text, even though the former was used in the title of "The Skater's March" added to the British Library's copy of the 1780 edition and throughout the 1797 edition, which included a new letter from the editor. Both "The Skater's March" (page 83) and the letter (page 91) are included in this edition.

Aside from these minor points, the book did not change much until the nineteenth century. The plates and parts of the text were updated in 1823, and Cormack substantially revised that version for the 1855 edition. I have ignored minor changes in wording, which generally served to make the text more concise, described small changes in content and organization in footnotes in the main text, and put new and substantially revised sections in the "Later Additions" part of this book (starting on page 107). My aim was to provide a useful edition for people interested in skating history who are more likely to be interested in the content of the book than its language.

I have also reorganized the explanatory material and added sections on all the editions of the book and on Jones's skates. Unless otherwise noted, translations and footnotes are my own. New captions have been added, and the figures have been renumbered. Figure and page number references have been updated to match this edition. Superscripted symbols reference footnotes in the original that are reprinted at the bottom of the page. Superscripted numbers reference endnotes printed starting on page 121.

A Treatise on Skating

— They sweep,
On sounding Skates, a thousand different ways,
In circling poize, swift as the winds.
Thomson.[1]

To the Right Honourable Lord Spencer Hamilton.

My Lord,
No one, who has had the pleasure of seeing your Lordship upon the ice, will ask why I was ambitious to prefix your name to the following Treatise. — I have often considered it as a blunder in many of our best authors, that they have dedicated their works to men, who, though conspicuous for their rank and fortunes, were however wholly unacquainted with the subjects which were in this manner put under their protection. — If any one should affect to despise the reputation of excelling in this amusement; I would wish them to consider, that merit is due to excellence of every kind; that the antients paid the highest regard to all those exercises which contributed to strength and activity; the faculties of the mind generally improving with those of the body. — Could we trace all great men through every period of their lives, we should find in the early part of them, that they discovered in their juvenile diversions the sparks of those qualities for which they became eminent when called to more serious and important occupations. Cæsar, or Alexander, would have dreaded as much, when they were boys, to have been outdone in swimming, running, or leaping, &c. as they would afterwards the loss of a battle; and whenever you, my Lord, shall be called forth to those employments which your birth and abilities demand, I may

venture to prophecy that you will appear as remarkable in the execution of them, as you are now for every elegant and genteel accomplishment.

I have the honour to subscribe myself,
My Lord,
Your Lordship's
Most obedient,
obliged humble servant,
Robert Jones

Preface

We have the happiness of living in so enlightened an age, that every thing is now reduced to a system. Essays and treatises have been written upon every art, from Machiavel on Government, down to the ingenious Mr. Savigny upon the use of the Razor. I mean not, by this expression, to depreciate the latter of these writers; for, if the merit of any composition is to be estimated by the benefit which mankind in general receive from it, there is no one but will prefer the writings of our countryman to those of the Italian. I own, that in this present treatise I labour under one difficulty, which is, that of not being able, like most modern authors, to trace my subject back to former ages, and illustrate it with quotations from the Greek and Roman authors: but if there should be any of my readers so much in love with antiquity, as to relish nothing but what was practised by our forefathers, I have it very luckily in my power to gratify them, by an extract from the works of Fitzstephen, a Monk in Henry the Second's time.

> When (says he) that great moor which washed Moorfields, at the North Wall of the city, is frozen over, great companies of young men go to sport upon the ice, and bind to their shoes bones,[2] as the legs of some beasts; and hold stakes in their hands, headed with sharp iron, which sometimes they flick against the ice; and these men go on with speed, as doth a bird in the air, or

darts shot from some warlike engine; sometimes two men set themselves at a distance, and run one against another, as it were at tilt, with these stakes, wherewith one or both parties are thrown down, not without some hurt to their bodies; and after their fall, by reason of their violent motion, are carried a good distance one from another; and wheresoever the ice doth touch their heads, it rubs off the skin, and lays it bare; and if one fall upon his leg or arm, it is usually broken; but young men, being greedy of honour, and desirous of victory, do thus exercise themselves in counterfeit battles that they may bear the brunt more strongly when they come to it in good earnest.[3]

And even so early as in the fifteenth century,[4] we may find that this art arrived to some degree of perfection in Holland, from the manner in which it is mentioned by Tasso,

> Sì come sogloin là vicino el polo,
> S'avien, che'l verno i fiumi agghiacci e indure,
> Correr sei'l ren le villanelle à stuolo
> Con lunghi strisci, e sdrucciolar secure.
> Gierusalemme liberata
Canto 14.[5]

It may be no small recommendation of skating, that it is practised in those seasons, when scarce any other exercise out of doors can be used with safety: but, besides this, nothing can be imagined more conducive to the health or spirits; and I am sure from experience it is an excellent preservative against the gout, a circumstance which I am surprized has escaped the notice of Doctor Cadogan: I hope he will do me the justice of mentioning it in his next edition.[6]

It has been suggested to me, that, in the present age, those diversions only meet with approbation, which bring the sexes most effectually together; and skating is calculated only for the male part of our species. This objection would have some weight, were it true: but, for my own part, I see no reason why the ladies are to be excluded; to object to it as not being hitherto practised, is the effect of prejudice and confined ideas: the same spirit which established the Coterie may make this as fashionable a diversion for one sex as the other. No motion can be more happily imagined for setting off an elegant figure to advantage; nor does the minuet itself afford half the opportunity of displaying a pretty foot: a lady may indulge herself here in a *tête a tête* with an acquaintance, without provoking the jealousy of her husband; and should she unfortunately make a slip, it would at least not be attended with any prejudice to her reputation.

SKATES may be had, after the Author's Plan, at RIC-CARD's Manufactory, at the Corner of *Orange Court*, next the *Mews Gate, Castle Street.*

Section I

Of the different methods of fixing on skates

Various methods have been made use of, to fasten on the skates; some have done this by means of a strong tape put through the holes in the front of the skate, which is then tied across the toes, and from thence being carried through the rings in the heel strap, is brought back again, and tightly fastened by a knot, over the instep; some have their shoes screwed to the stocks of skates; others have them fastened to plates of brass, which are fixed to the skate irons, instead of wooden stocks: there is also another method practised by many, which is, the having a piece of plate iron fixed across the stock at the heel, and a piece of the same sort on the tread, these pieces of iron have their end turned up; that on the tread:[7] to fit over the edges of the shoe soles; and the other over the heel, to which the iron is screwed on both sides.

The method which is taken by the common people is so well known, as not to need any particular description; they only make use of buckles, straps, rings, and heel pegs*; which method may be well enough for those who continue this diversion for a few minutes at a time, and think skating consists in an awkward shuffling over the ice, for ten or a dozen yards, for they seldom or ever are able to go any greater length without falling, or at

---

*Quadrilateral pyramids of iron, about three quarters of an inch in length, joining to the head of the heel screws.

least being obliged to stop to re-tighten their skates, which by this method of fastening are continually getting loose: as they are prevented from slipping behind, by means of the heel pegs before-mentioned, so they endeavour to keep them steady at the toe, by means of small pieces of iron, so sharply pointed as to enter easily into the sole of the shoe. I have made repeated tryals of all the above methods of fastening the skate, but have found none of them succeed to my satisfaction; and I think the reasons why they do not are pretty obvious. Tape never can be made a proper fastening; as it is liable to stretch, the knot tied with it must be continually growing slack: to obviate this defect, it is stretched to the utmost tightness it will bear, so that the blood vessels and tendons of the feet are so violently pressed, that a numbness, or cramp, is in general the consequence; another objection to tape is, that, by its fretting against the soles of the shoes, it oftentimes breaks on a sudden, which accident if it should happen to a person skating with any degree of velocity, the consequence may be fatal.

When the shoes are screwed to the stocks, as mentioned in the second method, the skates have no proper play; for, unless the shoes be large, the ankles will run great risk of being sprained by the sudden jirks of the skates, which often happens in going over rough ice; if the shoes be too large, the feet will then have so much play, that the motion must be irregular and uneasy.

As to the third method, where the stocks are made

of brass, the same objection will lye as to the second; and they will have this defect, that the stocks may be easily broken.

In the last method, we find the skates are screwed by pieces of iron being fixed across the stocks, which produces almost the same bad effects as screwing on the shoes: this method is likewise very dangerous; for, on any extraordinary inclination of the body sideways, the iron on the tread may touch the ice, and, by not being pliable, prevent the shoe from bending, and throw the skate off its edge; or, by sticking in the ice, be forced either from the stock or from the shoe.

The method of fastening on skates, with straps at the toes and heels, has long been approved of, by most skaters who have not arrived to great perfection; it is certainly the best method yet known, for plain skating and travelling, because the skates and feet have sufficient play, and are no ways constrained. The reason why this method is only fit for plain skating, and travelling, is on account of the following defect, namely, that in any other sort of skating, where sudden and irregular motions are made use of, the peg will come out of the heel of the shoe, and cause a fall.

All the preceding methods being defective in some particular or other; I shall now give one both safe and simple, which I have practised for many years, without the least inconveniency. My method is this: Let the skates be prepared with toe and heel straps, as usual; but instead of heel pegs, let the heel screws be made with flat heads, and long enough to go through the heels of the shoes, in which holes must be bored, and the heads of the screws sunk even with the leather, to prevent hurting the feet; to guard against which more effectually, let a piece of leather be sewed to the quarter of the shoe, large enough to cover the whole heel, which will defend it sufficiently from the screw.

The reader will easily conceive what advantage this method has over all those before mentioned, from the following observations: First, by the screw going through the lifts of the heel, the skate is prevented from altering its position in that part; secondly, when those sort of heel screws are used, the straps are not required to be drawn so tight as to give pain to the feet: I have made, it is true, an objection before, to fastening the shoe to the skates without straps; but this method of screwing them at the heel has by no means the same bad effect; for, the screws being in the centre, and the leather pliable, the shoes have their liberty at the sides. I have found by experience, that the skate must not be confined at the toes, and yet that it is necessary to prevent it there also from slipping. The points of iron on the tread are continued for that purpose.

Of the construction of skates

I will venture to say, those who have skated in England and in Holland, or have made use of English and Dutch skates, will give the preference to those made after the English fashion; not that it is fair to condemn the construction of Dutch skates, as that nation makes use of them chiefly for travelling; and here indeed they exceed ours; for, by reason of their great length, flat and broad surface, they run over rough ice with ease and expedition; their irons are likewise made low, consequently not so heavy as the English: ours would by no means be proper for travelling, because the irons are short and circular; not above two inches of their surface touch the ice at a time;[8] all our attention is required, to keep the body in an equilibrium on so small a base, which would be almost impossible to continue for any length of time; and the weight of the irons would add to the fatigue.

The Dutch, finding by experience that the length and straightness of their skate irons increased the friction upon the ice, have of late years made them shorter and more curved. Skating among the Dutch, is not so much an exercise or diversion, as business and necessity; the nature of their country and the continuance of their frosts make it so; consequently, safety and expedition is all they have to consider; and I have before shewn that this is sufficiently attended to, in the formation of their skates. In England, the case is different; skating is used here as an exercise and diversion only; hence an easy movement and graceful attitude are the sole objects of our attention. To arrive at these, nothing can be better imagined than the present form of our skates.

The reason we differ from them in the make of our skates is, that most of the graceful attitudes and movements are performed on the outside edges, with variety of curved lines; some of which being made infinitely short, if the irons were not of a circular form, it would be impossible to turn in so small a space: as this circular form accelerated the motion, and was the first improvement on Dutch skates, so the lowness of the iron was soon found to be an hindrance to a proper inclination of the body. Hence their height was increased, which alteration answered extremely well, particularly in assisting the long roll, which before could not be done in a proper and becoming position.[9]

These amendments and alterations being made with so much success, many others soon followed, which would be difficult and tedious to explain by words only: I shall therefore refer the reader to the Plates. Figure 3 (top) represents a skate, made after the English fashion, with some improvements; the proportions are as follows: Let the distance from the point of the fender, A, to the toe hook,* which is shewn by the pricked line, be one inch, and three quarters; B, the fort of the iron, whose lower surface is five sixteenths of an inch in breadth, and gradually increases to five eighths of an inch, at the point of the fender; and from B, must gradually decrease to a bare quarter of an inch, at the heel D.[10] C, the arch where the height of the iron is one inch three eighths; at B, one inch one eighth; and at D, one inch and a quarter: the groove that is cut in the stock, to receive the upper edge of the iron, is seldom made more than a quarter of an inch deep, so that the height of the iron from the stock will be at the arch one inch and one eighth, which is high enough for any sort of skating. E, the toe strap hole; F, the under strap hole;

---

*This hook is made of the same piece with the skate iron; it goes into the stock at the toe, over the strap hole, to keep the iron and stock together.

each of these holes must be cut so that the straps may go in very tight. G, the heel peg, whose diameter at bottom is a quarter of an inch, and at top one eighth; its height is determined by the heel of the shoe with which it is to be worn, but is seldom less than half an inch. H, the heel screw, which should always be made short.

Figure 3 (bottom) is a plan of a skate compleat, with straps, &c. M, the heel of the stock, whose diameter is two inches and three eighths. G, the waist, whose diameter is one inch one eighth. L, the tread, which is two inches and seven eighths in breadth. The thickness of the stock is three quarters of an inch; but the surface of the tread must be depressed a quarter of an inch, that the ball of the foot may rest easy.

I. I. I. are little sharp points of iron, each of which projects from the stock about one eighth of an inch; the distance from the centre of the under strap hole, to the extremity of the heel, is two inches and a half; and from the centre of the heel peg, A, to the extremity of the heel, one inch one eighth; K, the under strap; P, the heel strap, N. N. rings to which the straps are sewed; the length of the under strap from ring to ring is five inches and a half, and the heel strap seven inches; the length of the toe strap is determined by the size of the foot, but it must always sit very tight in the stock.

N. B. These proportions are for a middle-sized foot.

I have said nothing of those skates whose surfaces are grooved, and are commonly called fluted skates,[11] because I think their construction is so bad, that they

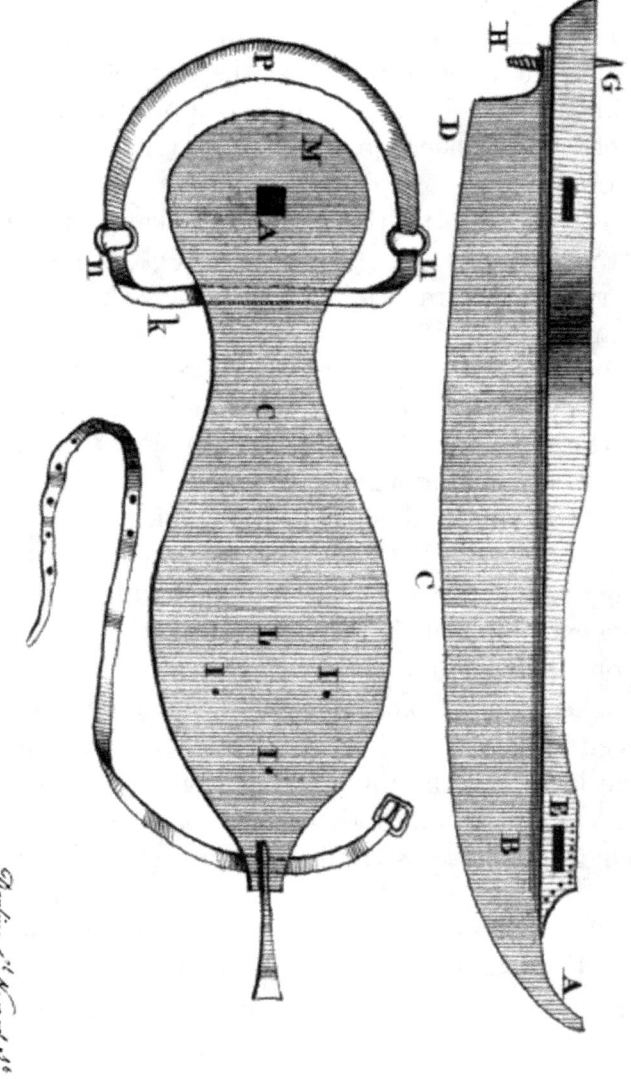

Figure 3: Two views of an English skate (1772).

are not fit to be used; in fact, they are so generally disapproved of, that I shall dispense with explaining their defects.[12]

Of the first position

Having fixed on the skates, according to any of the preceding methods, or in what manner you like best, place your heels together, with the toes inclining outwards; then lift up the left foot, without bending the instep, and put it down again in the same position, with your heel facing the ball of the right foot, at six inches distance; then with a small force throw your body forwards, bending at the left knee a little more than in common walking; at the same time you throw yourself forwards, strengthen the right knee, so that you may press on the inside edge of the skate, and force yourself forwards on the left leg; this method must be observed with both legs, and is called a Stroke.

As it would be difficult for beginners to continue long on one leg; which to attempt, they would get many falls; therefore I would advise them, to make their strokes as short as possible.

There[13] are, besides these instructions for managing the feet, others as necessary for the head and arms; which in skating must cooperate with the legs. It is remarkable that learners throw their arms about carelessly, or in a wild manner, as if they were catching at something to prevent their falling; which is the very means of throwing them down: the body being supported on so small a base as the edge of the skate, the poize is very difficult to attain, and I believe equal to that of walking on the tight rope, in which it is seen how essential the arms are, in preserving a proper balance; on the same principle, the arms act in skating, serving as a counterpoise when they are moved; and if they are not properly disposed, it will be impossible to stand, on either the out or inside edge, with any certainty. At first, the arms should be held out before, where they may be used to assist the body; but if you throw one of them behind in going on, you will find it immediately retard your motion, as well as alter your intended course.

The head should also[14] be held still; but as that is rather difficult at first, you may move it from side to side as often as you change your feet, and let the eyes be fixed on the fender of the skate you are moving:[15] in changing the feet in order to make a new stroke, the motion must not be the same as in walking, which is a thing that often escapes young[16] beginners; who are often observed, when changing their feet, to bend the knee only, and lift their legs up too high behind them; when on skates, we have not the power of rising on the toes, nor of even bending the knee, as we do in walking, where we are obliged to rise ourselves upon the toes of one foot, in order to bring the other forward, without its touching the ground; for want of making these observations, young[17] beginners make no difference between skating and walking, in the use of their legs; forgetting that they cannot bend the joints of their feet, nor rise on the toes, as they endeavour to do; which causes their feet to slip up so suddenly behind, and which not only appears very aukward, but hinders them from performing any one stroke they attempt. With great pains indeed and long labour, many insensibly arrive to a tolerable proficiency; but this they might have acquired in half the time, with a very little trouble, had they received proper instructions at first.

As we have explained the difference between skating and walking, and proved that the feet cannot act in both alike; it is proper next to teach in what manner you must act, to supply the place of bending the feet; which may be done, by lifting the knees considerably higher than in walking; and putting them down bent, and with a stiff instep (as before directed), so that the irons of the skate may always come down parallel to the ice; which method must be followed on all occasions, with this difference only, that they are sometimes put down flat, and sometimes on their edges, according to the stroke intended.

The rules which I have here laid down, are much more necessary for grown persons than for youth: the latter, beginning with spirit and resolution, scramble on in a careless manner, not regarding a few falls, which seldom affect them: in grown persons, the case is different; their joints are not so pliable as easily to be bent into various positions; and whenever they fall, they come down with such violence as often proves fatal.[18] The first position is nothing more than learning to stand firm on the ice; which having learned, you are properly prepared to proceed with the more agreeable part of the art; for the first position may be said to be only a preparative to skating, as turning out the toes is to dancing.[19]

Of the inside edge

As most people fall into this manner of skating before they attempt any other, I shall lay down some plain rules, by which it may be learned with ease and certainty in a very short time.

Let it then be remembered, that nature may be almost always improved; and that whatever contributes towards that improvement, ought not to be esteemed trifling or unnecessary: the inside edge is sometimes required, in performing some of the more difficult manœuvres; therefore it ought not to be forgot, nor neglected, as it is by many, when they have learned to go on the outside; not reflecting within themselves, that the perfection of every art depends on its first principles; and to attain true perfection, all its different branches must concur.

When you have learned to stand firm, and to move about, without falling; the method of proceeding, in order to gain the inside edge, is this: supposing you would make a stroke with the right foot, you must, as soon as your foot sets off, lift up the left foot behind the right, with the toe inclining downwards, at about six or seven inches distance from the right heel, and with the fender[20] two or three inches from the ice; this position of the left leg, with the head at the same time turned to the left, the right arm a little bent, and held out on the right side nearly as high as the shoulder, and the left arm held still close to the side, will cause you to make a sweep to the left on the inside edge. This position reversed, will carry you with a sweep on the left leg to the right; in going on the inside edge, keep the instep stiff, so as not to bend on either side; your observing this attitude will always bring you on the inside edge, though you should begin the stroke on the flat. When you have practised these rules, so as to be able to keep your poize on the edge, and to make long and short strokes at pleasure, and with certainty; you may next proceed to travelling, which we will next treat of.

Of travelling on the inside edge

Travelling* on the inside edge is by no means pleasant, nor is it often practised by those who are further advanced in skating: yet it is sometimes necessary, to relieve, when we are tired of going on the outside edge; which, though an agreeable motion, and pleasing to the spectator, is fatiguing if continued long without changing to the inside.

It is amazing what relief is given, by changing from one edge to the other, in going a journey of forty or fifty miles, which is frequently done in Holland and many other countries; and sometimes twice that distance in one day. Perhaps some of our English skaters will despise learning the inside edge, because it is not

---

*By travelling, is not meant going on a journey, as the common use of the word seems to imply, but a term for a particular movement on the skates.

a graceful attitude, and that they have no occasion to make such long journies; therefore would rather chuse to travel on the outside edge, as it is more pleasing.

Tho' these objections may be made, and perhaps appear reasonable to the unexperienced; yet, I would not advise any one to neglect making himself master of the inside edge, before he attempts proceeding any further; by the help of which, he will not only be able to roll sooner, but with more ease; because the finishing of every roll is on the inside edge.

That changing from one method of travelling to the other, must give relief, is obvious; and may be proved by any one action of our bodies, which, if continued to a certain time, becomes tiresome, the tone of the muscles and sinews being strained.

The reason why it is necessary, in skating, to alter our attitude pretty frequently, is, that every motion, being in æquilibrio, is consequently more fatiguing when we do not depend on so nice a poize.

Having theoretically proved the utility of travelling on the inside edge; I shall proceed with giving such instructions, as, if duly observed, any person may easily become master of the same. When you have made yourself perfect on the inside edge, and on both legs alike; begin to travel in this manner: Having put one foot down, to make a stroke, so far advanced, that the distance from the heel to the toe of the other foot be about twelve inches; set off on the flat of the skate, and gradually incline to the inside edge: we will suppose this stroke to be made on the right foot, with no other assistance than the pressure of the body; by this method, it would be impossible to travel fast; which to do, you must force yourself on with the other foot, as described in page 45; and directly upon the beginning of the stroke raise the left foot, about eight inches behind the right heel: this position must be continued till you change the stroke on the other leg; which must be done according to the preceding directions, reversed: a succession of these strokes, made alternately, will accelerate your motion, in proportion to the curves you form; and the distance of time, in going any determined distance, will be as the curvature of the lines of direction you move in: as curves thus made are indefinite, I shall not pretend to give any particular form of them;[21] instead of which, let us describe a channel or road, in order to regulate the curves or sweeps in the best manner for expeditious travelling.

Suppose a journey of ten miles, to be performed by two skaters, who shall move with equal velocity, one on a road six feet broad, which is described by the lines below, 1, 2, 3, 4, Fig. 4; and the other on a road eight feet broad, as described by the lines 5, 6, 7, 8, Fig. 5.

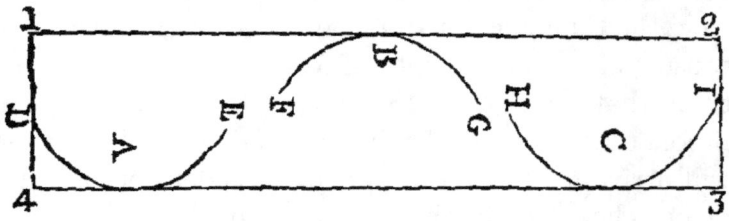

Figure 4: A journey on a road six feet broad (1772).

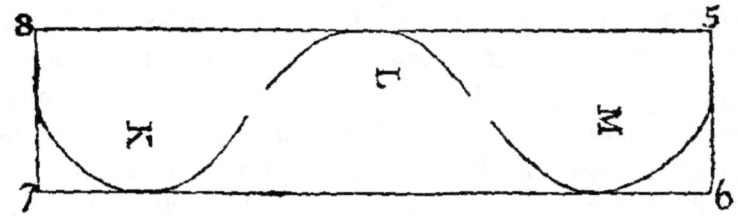

Figure 5: A journey on a road eight feet broad (1772).

In figure 4, the curve lines A, B, C, represent the lines of direction; A, a stroke made on the right foot, from D to E; B, the second stroke on the left foot, from F to G; C, the third on the right foot, from H to I: in this manner the curves are formed, between the lines 1, 2, 3, 4, alternately, from one foot to the other.

Again, we will suppose another skater, forming the curves K, L, M, in Fig. 5, and moving with the same velocity as the former in Fig. 4. We shall find that the different times of performing their journey will be as the length and flexure of the curves they describe, which curves will differ according to the breadth of the roads. Now the difference of time cannot be ascertained, bacause[22] of the uncertainty of forming the curves: yet I think that the figures already described, give sufficient proof, that the traveller in the road of six feet broad will arrive at his journey's end in a considerable time before the other in the road of eight feet broad. Although what has been said may be conceived on first sight of the figures, and any further demonstration dispensed with; yet, according to the rules of art, we must proceed, in a regular manner, to prove the most trifling proposition.

It[23] would be somewhat difficult for any one to know, when he is travelling, whether he makes his road six or eight feet broad, the breadth being intirely imaginary: but let this rule be observed; which is, always to make the sweeps as straight as possible, the more so the better; and the more direct the course, the less will be the resistance and friction; which sufficiently proves that narrow roads are best.

In travelling on the inside edge, the head and arms are not to be used in the same manner as in beginning to skate. The manner in which they should be employed may easily be conceived, being no other than that position in which they are held at the beginning of a minuet, only that the arms should be a little more advanced; and if they are suffered to hang with freedom, their motions will be governed by those of the body, which I think is the most graceful way they can be employed: the head must incline from side to side, gradually, as the stroke is changed, always looking forward to the way you are going.

The above instructions, followed with attention, added to a little practice, will soon make every motion become easy and familiar, and to seem in a manner natural.

Of the outside edge

Young[24] beginners will be a little surprized, when they find they have not yet come to that movement, which appears so agreeable to the eye, and which they are all so ambitious of attaining; and imagine, by the preceding instructions, that there is more difficulty in their way than they are aware: but they may be assured, that it will be easier in practice than it appears in theory.

I hope what has been said, will give the reader sufficient encouragement, to attend with patience to the following instructions; which, when put in practice, will give full satisfaction for the disagreeable time spent in learning the first principles.

To preserve the balance on the outside edge, requires more skill than any of the former positions; and is so difficult to be acquired, that I have known many to spend three or four winters in learning it. This I can impute to no other cause than their not having pursued a proper method at first setting out. It is common for those who first attempt moving on the outside edge, to inquire of others, in what manner they must begin; and upon not finding themselves immediately succeed, attribute it to the fault of their advisers; and apply to some others, for different instructions: these instructions being generally different, and the learner not having a proper perseverance to continue his attempts, but continually changing from one method to another; is the reason we see so very few arrive at any perfection, on the outside edge.[25]

A Treatise on Skating

To prevent these disappointments, I will lay down one general rule, which I have never known to fail, even with those who at first seem the most aukward.

Suppose a stroke to be made on the left leg; it must be put down on the flat, with the knee bent, the head inclined to the left, the right arm held out nearly upon a line with the shoulder; and the left arm held close to the side: then, with the right foot, impel yourself to the left, by often pressing the inside edge of the skate on the ice; the left foot is not to be taken off: by this method, you will make a sweep, which you must endeavour to increase, by inclining the body to the left; and bearing on the outside edge of the skate, and by gradually increasing your inclination, and turning the head more and more to the left shoulder, you will form a spiral line: this method must be reversed, for the right leg; and if practised for two or three days, the outside edge may be acquired.

The impellent foot being wholly employed at first learning the outside, no regard is paid to its position during the intervals of each stroke: but when the outside is acquired, it must then be thus disposed of. Suppose a stroke to be made on the left leg, raise the right leg behind, by bending the knee only; which knee must not be more than three or four inches from the left ham, and the foot hung down in an easy manner, with the toe downwards, within two or three inches of the ice.

When you can follow this method with both legs, and change the position of the arms with the stroke, you will then be prepared for travelling; which I shall treat of next.

Of travelling on the outside edge

This sort of travelling is thought to be more pleasing and expeditious than any other: it is the method which the Dutch chiefly make use of, in performing their long journeys, sometimes with heavy loads balanced upon their heads.

They travel on the outside edge, with their hands in their side pockets; this position of the arms I would recommend, as the most easy: but for expedition, they must be held forwards, and used occasionally to assist the motion; in what particular manner they are to be employed on such occasions, experience will teach best; for most people differ in the manner of using their arms when going fast on the ice, as they do when running on the ground; to strike on the outside edge, has already been taught; but to travel on the outside, you must make strokes alternately with both legs: and at every stroke, let the impellent foot be held, nearly parallel to the other, at about twelve inches distance, for about two or three paces; and then brought up suddenly to the other, in order to make a new stroke; the faster you would go, the farther the foot must be advanced in taking the strokes; but to move slowly and gracefully, it must be put down, with the heel at a little distance from the toe of the other foot.

The head is governed by the changing of the legs, and must be gradually moved from side to side, so that you may always look in the same direction with the curve you make; to be more explicit, the whole body and head must be inclined alternately from one side to the other, with as much ease and regularity as possible. When all these motions become familiar, travelling at a moderate rate will not be in the least fatiguing.

To travel very fast, the strokes must be made as short, and the curves as nearly approaching to right lines, as possible.[26]

Of the curved line on the outside edge, called rolling

This sort of skating, performed by a person of a genteel figure,[27] is the most graceful and becoming movement of all others; and must appear to those who neither consider, nor understand, the reason of the body's being preserved so long in a falling state, as it were somewhat amazing: but, if mechanically considered, it may easily be conceived, with this allowance, that nature here, as well as on many occasions, acts in a manner that cannot be intirely reduced to mechanical principles. This may be proved, by supposing a figure of a man, made of wood; and that the centre of gravity in such a figure was in the same point as it is said to be in the human body; in which it is situated in the middle between the two hips, or in that part called the Pelvis. Now suppose the figure to stand erect, with the feet placed parallel to each other, within a square of twelve inches; then, if a perpendicular be let fall from the centre of gravity, it will meet the ground nearly in the middle of the square: but if the body be inclined any way, so that the perpendicular should not touch the ground in the centre of the square, the figure will immediately fall, even supposing the limbs moveable, and placed in the best manner for preserving the poize: in the human body the case is different; which I have found by experience, that a man may stand, though he be so inclined, that the perpendicular should fall at the toes (provided he has the proper use of his limbs). I can assign no other reason for his being capable of supporting himself in such an attitude, than the wonderful construction, and manner of acting of the muscles.

By the preceding remarks as well as by the following instructions, we shall find that skating manœuvres are mechanically performed; rolling, ought not to be learned in a hurry, nor with both legs, till you are perfect on one; and it is difficult to roll well, after you have contracted a bad habit, which is always the consequence of learning too soon on both legs. This I have observed in many, who, though they were firm on their skates, could not move equally well on both legs.

Rolling must be learned in this manner. Take a step with the left foot, putting it down flat, at about ten inches from the ball of the right foot; and let the toe be turned pretty much out: incline the body forwards, and the head to the left, directing the eyes that way; let the arms be easily crossed over the breast; some chuse to let them hang down at their sides, and others put them behind their backs: both these methods are straining, and not graceful.

At setting off, the left knee must be a little bent, and gradually straightened, as you move, till it is quite straight; which it must be at the end of the curve. The right leg must be slowly raised behind, with the toe out, and pointing downwards: this leg serves as a counterpoize to the inclining body; when you have made about half the sweep, bring the right leg slowly forward, in order to take another stroke, in the same manner as with the left, only that the motions and positions must be reversed; in rolling fast, you must force yourself on with the impellent foot: but for slow rolling, the inclination of the body will be sufficient; to what height the leg is to be raised behind, cannot be determined, that depending intirely on the size of the curve; that is, the larger the curve, the higher the leg must be raised: but in common rolling, the toe need not be above three or four inches from the ice. The figure in the second plate [figure 6] represents a proper attitude for genteel rolling.[28]

Of running

Running is absolutely necessary in performing some of the masterly parts of this art; without which, it would be impossible to make the movements sufficiently large; any tolerable skater could run, were he not afraid of falling; which most are, because such sort of skating appears wild and dangerous; and indeed is so in those who attempt running in the same manner as on the ground. That those who choose to be masters of such manœuvres as are facilitated by running, may not be discouraged in their attempts; I will give such instructions, that they may venture without danger of falling.

It may be observed of skaters in general, who attempt to run, that, instead of doing so, they rather keep slid-

Figure 6: Common rolling (1772).

Figure 7: Rolling (1823).

Figure 8: Common rolling (1855).

ing along, with their feet nearly parallel, and often fall: the cause of their falling is, that they cannot stop the foremost foot, in order to take a step with the other; for the skate, moving forward in a right line, can have no hold on the ice, to check the motion; so that when the other foot is brought forward, that on which you are moving immediately slips back. The principal intent of running, is to add to the force of the body. Whenever we are desirous to make a very large roll or circle, &c. in the same manner as in leaping on the ground; we find ourselves assisted by running: but the above described method of doing this would not assist the velocity of the body, because, the skates having no hold of the ice (as was before observed), it would be difficult to stop, so as to make a spring, at the beginning of any manœuvre. If the following method be observed by a good skater, he may run as firm, and leap nearly as high with skates as without. In running, take short steps, turn out the toes, as much as you can with ease, and bring down each foot on the inside edge; at every step, strike on the ice, in the same manner as if you were stamping on the ground, and let the heel of the iron touch the ice first; the arms must be used as they are in running on the ground, the body inclined forwards, the head kept still, and the eyes fixed on the spot where you intend setting off with the spiral line, circle, &c.

Many accidents happen upon the ice, from the skaters running violently against each other; which is only to be prevented by learning the method of stopping themselves suddenly. This, after they have acquired the art of running, may be easily done, by leaping up, and coming down with the feet parallel, at about twelve inches asunder, and turned as much as possible to the right or left; so that according to the seaman's phrase, the broad sides of the skates may be before you: when travelling, you may stop yourself, by only turning the feet to the right or left, as before described, and pressing on the inside edge of the foremost foot. By these methods you may avoid many dangers, such as banks of snow, broken ice, &c. But the method which skaters generally make use of to stop themselves, is by no means so certain; for as they only bear on the heels of their skates, they run a considerable distance before they stop, by which means they not only spoil the ice, but often break their skates; and, unless they perceive the danger at some distance, are not able to escape it.

Section II

Of the spiral line

In the preceding part of this work, I have endeavoured to lay down proper instructions, for plain skating, and graceful rolling; and shall now treat of the more masterly parts of this art, which cannot be attained by those who are not naturally active, and possessed of some genius. It is rather difficult to form a spiral line, and at first learning is generally attended with some falls, owing to the great inclination of the body; but more frequently to the skates having a dull edge.

To form a large spiral line, take a run about thirty yards; and when you begin the line, throw yourself with great force on the left leg on the outside edge, the knee bent, and the body inclining forwards as much as possible; the arms must be held in the same position as an archer is described drawing his bow; the right leg raised behind as high as you can with ease, with the knee bent so much, that, as you look over the left shoulder, you may see the foot; as you proceed gradually, raise the body, and drop the right leg, so that, when you finish the line, the body may be upright, and the legs brought together; then take a small roll on the right leg, but before you begin, drop the left hand on the hip, and advance the right higher than the head, keeping your eyes fixed upon it at the same time; this attitude has a pretty effect at the conclusion of the spiral line.

Of the inside circle

The[29] inside circle is the largest manœuvre on the skates: it is necessary to be learned, because it teaches the method of turning out the toes; without which many other movements could not be done: the circle is thus performed; first take a run; then spring off on[30] both legs, on the inside edges, with the right foot first, turning yourself to the left; let the feet be in a line with the body, and the distance from heel to heel about eighteen inches; the feet must be turned so much out, that the skates may make but one track on the ice; bear full on the right foot, but raise the heel of the left skate a little, to prevent its catching in the ice, and tripping you up; at first setting off, stoop, bend the knees, and look to the right: but as you go on, raise yourself slowly, and straighten the knees till you come quite upright; the heels must be gradually brought together, and the head turned by degrees to the left: the hands may be disposed of any way, so that they are kept still;[31] it is to be observed, that the larger you intend the circle, the longer you must look to the right; and the less the circle, the sooner you must look to the left.

If you would form a scroll or spiral line, instead of a circle, you must, at setting off, place the left foot, so that it may cut a track about four inches behind the right; and when you have gone a little way, bring the head to the left, and look down at the left foot: by this method you may cut a compleat scroll; at coming near the end of it, shrink in the body, and raise the

Figure 9: The inside circle (1855).

shoulders, which will give you a short and sudden turn. The circle and scroll may be done equally as well to the right, by reversing the motions.

Of the outside circle

I have seen but few who were capable of making this circle: the reason of which is, that it is both difficult and straining; but if once learned, you will then have such command of your skates, that hardly any jerk, or irregular motion, will throw you off your[32] balance.

As the performing of this circle is difficult, and[33] requires much practice, it is better at first not to attempt to make it either compleat or large: but begin by throwing yourself on both feet, on the outside edges, with the right foot first; let the force be just sufficient to carry you a few yards, at the same time making a full face to the left: both feet must be turned out so much that the toes may be a little farther back than the heels; let the space between the heels be about two feet; look to the right, quite over the shoulder; stoop, and bend the knees; keep on the outside edges, but raise the left heel a little; the left foot must not run in the same track with the right, but must be two or three inches advanced; the best position for the arms is, to hang them in an easy manner before you; if, after making some tryals, you can move a few yards on the outside curve, you may then attempt to make a large circle; which may be done by taking a run, to accelerate the motion.

A scroll may be cut, instead of a circle, by looking more over the right shoulder, and advancing the left foot farther than in making the circle.

Of the flying Mercury

After any one is master of the preceding manœuvres, he will find all the others to be very easy: as for example, to perform the attitude of a flying Mercury,[34] is nothing more than the spiral line, except that the arms are not employed in the same manner; the figure in plate III [figure 10],[35] represents the attitude on the right leg, and almost at the conclusion of the stroke;[36] but at the beginning the body must lean forwards pretty much, with the right hand pointing to the ice, and slowly raised with the body, till you are quite upright; when you would finish the stroke, bring down the left leg, and throw it suddenly up before you, at the same time bearing on the right heel; by which means you may spin round two or three times, in order to conclude the spiral line, which should always be formed when in the attitude of Mercury.

Of the fencing position

This[37] position, though pleasing to the eye, is somewhat difficult to perform; the manner of doing it is this: when you have taken a sufficient run to increase the velocity of the body, throw your feet in a right line on the flat of both skates,[38] with the right foot first; raise the left heel a little up, but tread flat on the right foot; the

Figure 10: The flying Mercury (1772).

Figure 11: The Mercury position (1823).

Figure 12: The flying Mercury (1855).

right arm must be held out nearly in a line with the shoulder, and the eyes fixed on the fingers of that hand: the body must be held as upright as possible, the breast held out, and the head back: all these positions must be well observed; otherwise it will be impossible to move in a right line, or to keep your balance. This attitude is represented by the figure in the fourth Plate [figure 13].[39]

Of the salutation

This is a manœuvre that cannot be exhibited, unless the performers skate equally well, and are masters of the inside circle, and rolling.

Suppose two skaters standing opposite each other, at about twenty feet asunder; then let them both make a sweep on their right legs, till they come near enough together to join their right hands, keeping them no longer joined than while they pass one another; when they must immediately turn themselves on their right feet, and strike off with an inside circle to the left, drawing their right legs in the same manner as in making a bow at the beginning of a minuet: at commencing the circle, the hat must be pulled off, and held down during the bow, which may be made according to fancy; at the conclusion of the bow, both must turn suddenly round on the left leg, which may be easily done by throwing the right leg up to the left; when, turning, the hats must be put on: by thus turning round, they will come face to face, as at first setting off.[40]

Figure 13: The fencing position (1772).

Figure 14: The fencing position (1823).

Figure 15: The fencing position (1855).

Of the serpentine line

The serpentine line may be made either on one leg, or both; the method of forming it on one leg is this: take a short run, to assist your motion; then strike off on the right leg, holding the right arm out in a line with the shoulder, the left leg up behind as in common rolling: the left arm may hang down at the side; at first setting out, make a curve to the right, but make it as straight as you can; when you have gone a few yards, turn your head to the left, and bear on the inside edge; bring the left foot forward, and turn the right arm to the left: keep in this position till you choose to go again to the right, which may be done by changing the attitude to the same as at first setting off. By this method a serpentine line may be formed, as long as you can continue your course on one leg.

To form a serpentine line on both legs, set off in the same manner as in making the inside circle;[41] then change to the position for the outside circle; thus changing from one to the other, a serpentine line may be formed, more or less curved, according to the fancy.

N. B. The arms must be held in the same manner as in the fencing attitude.

These manoeuvres plainly prove what I before said, that the perfection of every art depends upon its first principles; for in these are used almost all the positions before taught.[42]

Of travelling backwards

To[43] travel backwards, is rather a whimsical movement than either necessary or pleasant: but as there may be some who wish to attempt it, I will lay down the plainest instructions for it in my power. To make a stroke on the left leg, turn in the toe of the right foot; and press on the inside edge, to force yourself backwards; and lean forwards as much as you can; the same method must be followed for the other foot: this movement requires a great deal of practice; but when once you have learned the method of making the strokes, you will be able to go at a great rate.

To cut the figure of a heart on one leg

This is a pleasing manœuvre, and but lately known; it is difficult, though graceful if well done;[44] the method is as follows: first[45] set off, with a sweep on the outside, on the right leg; and when you think you have formed half the figure of a heart, which you will almost naturally do in common rolling, turn yourself suddenly half round; then throw yourself on the inside edge, and by looking to the right you will move backwards. This motion must be continued till you come to the place where you began the heart; it would be rather difficult to describe in what manner the arms should be used, nor is it necessary, because those who are such proficients as to attempt this manœuvre, will certainly know how to employ them.

There[46] in the are many other movements performed

on skates, besides those I have treated of; but, as they are neither graceful nor pleasing, I shall here conclude, by saying, those who can perform all the manœuvres mentioned in this treatise, will have no occasion for any further instructions.

FINIS.[47]

Later Additions

The Skater's March

This song was bound with the British Library's copy of the 1780 edition. It consists of two leaves from the 1782 edition of European Magazine, *according to the British Library's catalog entry. It may have been performed as early as 1774, according to a notice in the* Caledonian Mercury *(see figure 16 on page 89). The sheet music has been reset for this edition.*

Composed for the Skaters Club of Edinburgh. As Sung by Mess.rs Bannister and Wilson.

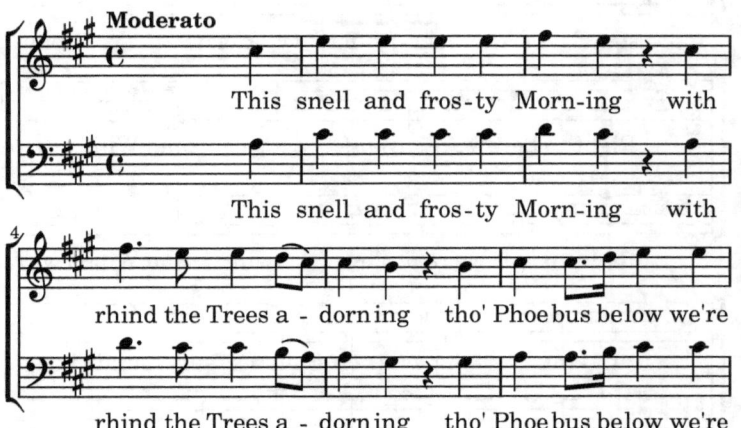

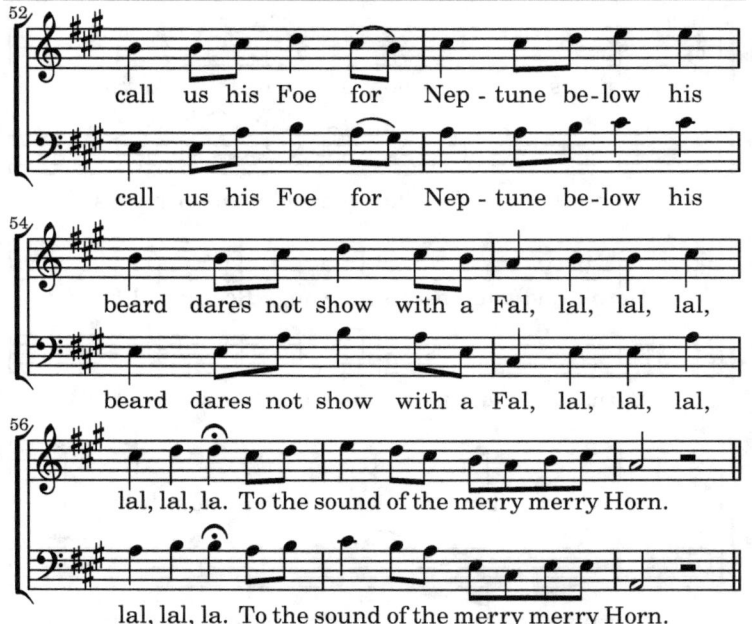

A Treatise on Skating

> **THEATRE ROYAL,**
> By HIS MAJESTY's SERVANTS,
> *By Desire of the Honourable The*
> **SKATING CLUB,**
> On WEDNESDAY next, will be performed
> The BEGGARS OPERA.
> Captain Macheath, Mr DIGGES.
> Lucy, Mrs Weston;—Polly, Mrs Rofs.
> Between the Play and the Farce will be sung, The
> **SKATERS MARCH.**
> By Mr Wilson, dress'd in the Uniform.
> To which will be added, a Farce, called
> **THE DUCE IS IN HIM.**
> Three rows of the Pit will be railed into boxes, for the
> Gentlemen of the Skating Club.
>
> On THURSDAY Next will be performed, the Tragedy of
> **VENICE PRESERV'D;**
> OR, A
> **PLOT DISCOVER'D.**
> Belvidera, by Mrs HUNTER.
> (Being her second appearance in that character.)
> Pierre,————Mr DIGGES.
> To which will be added, a New Speaking Pantomime, called
> The INVASION of HARLEQUIN;
> OR,
> **SHAKESPEAR TRIUMPHANT.**
> As performed at the Theatre Royal Drury Lane, with the
> greatest applause.
> Harlequin, Mr Mills; Simon, Mr Inchbald; Snip the taylor, Mr Mofs; Abram, Mr Death; Corporal Bounce, Mr Hague; Forge, Mr Webb; Frenchman, Mr Charteris; Welchman, Mr Hatton; Juftice, Mr Smith; Irishman, Mr Ward; Difmal, Mr Rofs.——Mercury, Mrs Rofs; Mrs Snip, Mrs Webb; Mifs Suky Chitterlin, Mrs Johnfon; Mifs Dolly Snip, by Mrs WESTON.
> VIVANT REX ET REGINA!

Figure 16: Announcement of a performance that included the Skater's March at the Theatre Royal in Edinburgh. Notice from the *Caledonian Mercury*, January 24, 1774, 3.

The editor to the reader

This letter and the following note about buying skates were included in the 1797 edition in place of the dedication and preface in the earlier editions.

The Editor of the following Edition of Jones's Treatise hath ventured to make a few alterations in it, as they are improvements in that very elegant art since that gentleman wrote his excellent book.

The new invented Half-Boot Skate is here offered to the public for the first time.[48] It is the iron part of the Skate, so fixed on the sole of the Half-Boot, as to need no wood work, or other fastening; the Boot is then laced, and a very tight brace from the heel buckles over the instep.

The inventor of this Skate never saw Mr. Jones's book: if it has an objection, it seems to be that of being fast at the toe, which Mr. Jones objects to:—but perhaps the play the foot has in the fore part of the Half-Boot may obviate this objection.—The Editor has found the plan, on trial, the best he has experienced.

The Dedication and Preface to the original work are omitted; the first being adulatory, and out of date, and the second an affectation of wit and learning, and applying in no way to advantage the student in this most graceful, delightful, and healthy amusement.

T. C. R.[49]

N. B. The new invented Half-Boot Skates above mentioned, are sold by the inventor, Mr. JAMES, No. 14, Newgate-Street, and by THOMAS OLIO[50] RICKMAN, No. 7, Upper Mary-le-bone Street.—Price *One Guinea and a Half.*

Preface to the 1823 edition

From 1823 onward, the book was published under the new title The Art of Skating *with some changes. The preface was revised, with the main change being the addition of several new paragraphs. These paragraphs and other changes are shown in blue.*

We have the happiness of living in so enlightened an age, that every thing is now reduced to a system. Essays and tTreatises have been written upon every art, from Machiavel on Government, down to the ingenious Mr. Savigny upon the use of the Razor. I mean not, by this expression, to depreciate the latter of these writers;, for, if the merit of any composition is to be estimated by the benefit which mankind in general receive from it, there is no one but will prefer the writings of our countryman to those of the Italian. I own, that in this present treatise I labour under one difficulty, which is, that of not being able, like most modern authors, to trace my subject back to former ages, and illustrate it with quotations from the Greek and Roman authors: b; for, it is certain that, although the ancients excelled in most athletic sports, skating seems to have been unknown to them. But if there should be any of my readers so much in love with antiquity, as to relish nothing but what was practised by our forefathers, I have it very luckily in my power to gratify them, by an extract from the works of Fitzstephen, a Monk in Henry the Second's time.

"When (says he) that great moor which washed Moorfields, at the North Wall of the city, is frozen over, great companies of young men go to sport upon the ice, and bind to their shoes bones, as the legs of some beasts; and hold stakes in their hands, headed with sharp iron, which sometimes they stick against the ice; and these men go on with speed, as doth a bird in the air, or darts shot from some warlike engine; sometimes two men set themselves at a distance, and run one against another, as it were at tilt, with these stakes, wherewith one or both parties are thrown down, not without some hurt to their bodies; and after their fall, by reason of their violent motion, are carried a good distance one from another; and wheresoever the ice doth touch their heads, it rubs off the skin, and lays it bare; and if one fall upon his leg or arm, it is usually broken: but young men, being greedy of honour, and desirous of victory, do thus exercise themselves in counterfeit battles that they may bear the brunt more strongly when they come to it in good earnest."

And even so early as in the fifteenth century, we may find that this art arrived to some degree of perfection in Holland, from the manner in which it is mentioned by Tasso,

A Treatise on Skating

Sì come sogloin là vicino el polo,
S'avien, che'l verno i fiumi agghiacci e indure,
Correr sei'l ren le villanelle à stuolo
Con lunghi strisci, e sdrucciolar secure.
Gierusalemme Liberata, Canto ~~14~~xiv.

It may be no small recommendation of skating, that it is practised in those seasons, when scarce any other exercise out of doors can be used with safety: but, besides this, nothing can be imagined more conducive to the health or spirits; and I am sure from experience it is an excellent preservative against the gout, a circumstance which I am surprized has escaped the notice of our doctors.

It[51] is not known when skating made its appearance in England, but, it is most probable, that as at present exercised, it was brought from the Low Countries, where it is said to have originated, and is much practised by all ranks of both sexes. The editors of the Encyclopædia Britannica tell us, that Edinburgh has produced more instances of elegant skaters than perhaps any other country whatever:[52] those, however, who have witnessed the rapidity and the dexterous evolutions of the London skaters, will be somewhat unwilling to yield the palm to Edinburgh. "I have seen," says Strutt,[53] "when the Serpentine River, in Hyde Park, was frozen over, four gentlemen there dance, if I may be allowed the expression, a double minuet in skates, with as much ease, and, I think, with more elegance than in a ball-room; others, again, by turning and winding with great adroitness, have readily in succession described upon the ice, the form of all the letters in the alphabet." It is this very adroitness, however, which forms the exception to the London style of skating; it wants that bold sweep which is an essential requisite of gracefulness in this agreeable recreation. The Edinburgh editors allow that the English are "remarkable for their feats of agility," and ascribe their deficiency in grace partly to the construction of their skates. "They are too much curved, it is said, in the surface which embraces the ice, consequently they involuntarily bring the users of them round on the outside upon a quick and small circle; whereas the skater by using skates less curved, has the command of his stroke, and can enlarge or diminish the circle, according to his own wish and desire.[54]

In America, as well as in Holland, skating is chiefly practised as an expeditious mode of travelling, when the rivers, canals, and lakes, are frozen up during winter, and celerity is there the great point aimed at. The expedition with which journeys may be made in this way, is extraordinary. A late Boston Gazette says, "Four young gentlemen belonging to Boston, travelled on skates a distance of nine miles in twenty-seven minutes, being at the rate of twenty miles in an hour. *Let any one in the world beat this if they can!*" The challenge was made with good reason; but great as was the feat, it was, if not surpassed, at least fully equalled, by a subsequent achievement of an English skater, who performed a mile in less than three minutes. The English performance was for a match of one hundred guineas. The skater was a countryman of the name of Githam, living in the neighbourhood of the

A Treatise on Skating

Cambridgeshire fens.[55] He started a few seconds before the time, and came up to the scratch at the moment appointed, and performed the distance in seven seconds within the three minutes.

Such speed is marvellous even when compared with that of the first race-horses. The Beacon course at Newmarket, is four miles round, and is rarely performed in less than seven minutes, fifteen or twenty seconds. The Flying Childers,[56] indeed, for a considerable wager, being put to his utmost speed from the moment of starting, accomplished it in five minutes and seventeen seconds; a rate of speed more than double that of the swiftest skating ever known.

It has been suggested to me, that, in the present age, those diversions only meet with approbation, which bring the sexes most effectually together; and skating is calculated only for the male part of our species. This objection would have some weight, were it true; but, for my own part, I see no reason why the ladies are to be excluded; to object to it as not being hitherto practised, is the effect of prejudice and confined ideas. The same spirit which established the Coterie may make this as fashionable a diversion for one sex as the other. No motion can be more happily imagined for setting off an elegant figure to advantage; nor does the minuet itself afford half the opportunity of displaying a pretty foot: a lady may indulge herself here in a *tête a tête* with an acquaintance, without provoking the jealousy of her husband; and should she unfortunately make a slip, it would at least not be attended with any prejudice to her reputation.

Revised 1823 preface

In the 1855 edition, the preface was revised once again. It was based on the preface to the 1823 edition and given the title "preface to the first edition". Changes from the 1823 version are given below in blue.

~~We have the happiness of living in so enlightened an age, that every thing is now reduced to a system. Essays and Treatises have been written upon every art, from Machiavel on Government, down to the ingenious Mr. Savigny upon the use of the Razor. I mean not, by this expression, to depreciate the latter of these writers; for, if the merit of any composition is to be estimated by the benefit which mankind in general receive from it, there is no one but will prefer the writings of our countryman to those of the Italian. I own, that in this present treatise I labour under one difficulty, which is, that of not being able, like most modern authors, to trace my subject back to former ages, and illustrate~~ There is a difficulty in tracing the subject of the present Treatise back to former ages, and illuminating it with quotations from Greek and Roman authors~~; f~~. For~~, it is certain that,~~ although the ancients excelled in most athletic sports, Skating seems to have been unknown to them. But ~~if there should be any of my readers so much in love with antiquity as to~~ parties who relish nothing but what was practised by our forefathers, ~~I~~

can fortunately be gratified by an extract from the works of Fitzstephen, a Monk, in Henry the Second's time.

> "When (says he) that great moor which washed Moorfields at the North Wall of the City is frozen over, great companies of young men go to sport upon the ice, and bind to their shoes bones of the legs of beasts, and hold stakes in their hands, headed with sharp iron, which sometimes they stick against the ice; and these men go on with speed as doth a bird in the air, or darts shot from some warlike engine. Sometimes two men set themselves at a distance and run one against the other, as it were at tilt, with those stakes, wherewith one or both parties are thrown down, not without some hurt to their bodies; and after their fall, by reason of their violent motion, are carried a good distance one from another; and wheresoever the ice doth touch their heads, it rubs off the skin and lays it bare; and if one fall upon his leg or arm, it is usually broken. But young men being greedy of honour, and desirous of victory, do thus exercise themselves in counterfeit battles, that they may bear the brunt more strongly when they come to it in good earnest."

And even so early as in the fifteenth century, we may

find that this art had arrived at some degree of perfection in Holland, from the manner in which it is mentioned by *Tasso*:—

> "Sì come sogloin là vicino el polo,
> S'avien, che'l verno i fiumi agghiacci e indure,
> Correr sei'l ren le villanelle à stuolo
> Con lunghi strisci, e sdrucciolar secure."
> *Gierusalemme Liberata*, Canto xiv.

It may be no small recommendation to Skating, that it is practised at a season when scarse any other exercise out of doors can be taken with safety; and nothing can be imagined more conducive to the health or spirits: and I am sure, from experience, it is an excellent preservative *against the gout*, a circumstance which I am surprised *has escaped* the notice of our *doctors*.

In Holland, Skating is much practised by both sexes. And there is no reason why, in a modified style, it should not be practised by the fair sex as a fashionable exercise. No motion can be more happily imagined for setting off an elegant figure to advantage, and for displaying a pretty foot.

The editors of the "Encyclopædia Britannica" tell us that Edinburgh has produced more instances of elegant Skaters than perhaps any other country. Those, however, who have witnessed the rapidity and the dexterous evolutions of the

London skaters, will be somewhat unwilling to yield the palm to Edinburgh. "I have seen," says Strutt, "when the Serpentine River in Hyde Park was frozen over, four gentlemen there dance, if I may be allowed the expression, a double minuet on skates, with as much ease, and I think with more elegance, than in a ballroom." It is the *adroitness*, which forms the exception to the London style of skating: it wants that bold sweep which is an essential requisite of gracefulness. The Edinburgh editors allow that the English are "remarkable for their feats of agility," and ascribe their deficiency in grace partly to the construction of their skates. These are too much curved, it is said, in the surface which embraces the ice; consequently they involuntarily bring the skater round on the outside upon a quick and small circle; whereas the skater, by using skates less curved, has the command of his stroke, and can enlarge or diminish his circle according to his wish.

In America, as well as in Holland, Skating is practised as an expeditious mode of travelling, when the rivers, canals, and lakes are frozen up. A Boston Gazette says, "Four young gentlemen belonging to Boston travelled on skates a distance of nine miles in twenty- seven minutes, being at the rate of twenty miles an hour. Let any one in the world beat this if he can!" But great as was the feat, it was, if not surpassed, at least fully equalled by a subsequent achievement of an

English skater, who performed a mile in less than three minutes. ~~The English performance was for a match of one hundred guineas.~~ The skater was a countryman~~,~~ of the name of Githam, living in the neighbourhood of the Cambridgeshire fens. He started a few seconds before the time, and came up to the scratch at the moment appointed, and performed the distance in seven seconds within the three minutes.

~~Such speed is marvellous even when compared with that of the first race-horses.~~ The Beacon Course of Newmarket~~,~~ is four miles round, and is rarely performed in less than seven minutes, fifteen or twenty seconds. The Flying Childers, indeed, for a considerable wager, being put to his utmost speed from the moment of starting, accomplished it in five minutes and seventeen seconds; a rate of speed more than double that of the swiftest skater ever known.

~~It has been suggested to me, that, in the present age, those diversions only meet with approbation, which bring the sexes most effectually together; and skating is calculated only for the male part of our species. This objection would have some weight, were it true: but, for my own part, I see no reason why the ladies are to be excluded; to object to it as not being hitherto practised, is the effect of prejudice and confined ideas: the same spirit which established the Coterie may make this as fashionable a diversion for one sex as the other. No motion can be more happily imagined for setting off an elegant figure to advantage; nor does the minuet itself afford half the opportunity of displaying a pretty foot: a lady may indulge herself here in a *tête a tête* with~~

an acquaintance, without provoking the jealousy of her husband; and should she unfortunately make a slip, it would at least not be attended with any prejudice to her reputation.

Preface to the 1855 edition

This section was added to the 1855 edition after the revised "Preface to the first edition" under the title "Preface to the present edition."

Presuming that our predecessor, Lieutenant R. Jones, R.A., who flourished some thirty years since, may be laid up with gout,[57] in consequence of the prevalence of mild winters, for some years past, having deprived him of the infallible "Gout Medicine"—Skating; and that he has not heard the loud calls, in 1852, for his Treatise, by those who have sound bones, and by those who have had them broken—we take the liberty of reviving his work without consulting him (for Frost will not wait for the result of consultation); and of engrafting upon it some additions to the art, which seem to have been acquired since he figured upon the living, ringing, buzzing Serpentine. Should our elder brother amateur be offended by our so doing, he is sincerely welcome, by way of amends, to the profits of the present revival of his genius.

Although there are *patent skates*, little has been written upon the use and application of them. What has not been published upon guns and *gunnery?* Horses and *horse-racing?* Fishing-rods and *angling?* Bats and *cricket?* Steam and electricity—and *their application* to create unity of *thought* and *humanity?* Yet how few have shone upon the subject of the ephemeral, cherubic sport, and highest order of gymnastic—*Skating?*

Until the Fair Sex participate more in the aerial recreation, for man to

"Behold a goddess" "on the crystal plane,"

the art of skating will never have arrived at perfection.

In 1801, two young women, going thirty miles in two hours, won the prize in a skating race at Groningen.

The following practical observations are intended or the skater of some proficiency rather than as a treatise upon skating.

Those who wish to peruse other papers on the subject, may be referred to the "Encyclopædias;" to the "Boy's Own Book, 1849," &c.

We hope that a more proficient amateur will speedily favour the skating world with a digested work to supersede the present brief and roughly got up pages, upon an advanced, yet imperfectly defined, art. Of the construction of skates—especially of their *fastenings*, including springs, &c., the advantages and disadvantages of certain approved forms—require to be further defined and *practically* determined—an *easy fitting skate* being to good skating a *sine qua non*.

New and revised instructions

This section highlights major changes W. E. Cormack made to Jones's original text when he republished it in 1855. Only sections that have been substantially revised or added are repeated here. Minor revisions are mentioned in endnotes instead.

Of the construction of skates, and the different methods of fixing them to the foot

Jones's first two chapters were combined and substantially revised in this section.

Those who have skated in England and in Holland, or have used English and Dutch skates, will give the preference to the former. Not that the construction of the Dutch skates is to be condemned, they being used in Holland chiefly for travelling, for which purpose they excel ours; their great length, flat and broad surface, fitting them to run over rough ice with ease and expedition. Their irons are likewise made low, consequently not so heavy as the English. Our irons being short and circular, a small portion only of their surface touches the ice at a time, and are therefore not so proper for travelling. Upon ours, the attention of the skater is more required to keep the body in an equilibrium on a small base, which is very laborious to continue for any length of time; and the weight of the irons adds to the fatigue.

The Dutch, finding by experience that the length and straightness of their skate-irons increased the friction upon the ice, now make them shorter and more curved.

In England, skating is used as an exercise and diversion only: hence, an easy movement and graceful attitude are the sole objects of our attention. To arrive at these, nothing has been better contrived than the present form of our Skates.

Most of the graceful attitudes and movements are performed on the outside edges, in a variety of curved lines; some of which, being made infinitely short, if the irons were not of a *circular* form, it would be impossible to turn in a small space. As this circular form accelerated the motion towards curvilinear lines, and was the first improvement in Dutch skates, so the lowness of the iron was soon found to be a hindrance to a proper inclination of the body, Hence their *height* or depth was increased; which answered particularly well in assisting the long roll, that before could not be done in a proper and becoming position.

The best formed skate *Iron*, for English skating, is that introduced of recent[58] years, that running the whole length of the stock, and flush with the stock at heel and toe, the toe end rounded underneath, like the runner of a sledge, or the stem of a ship.

Many of the London skaters have the irons rounded under the heel also; but, notwithstanding, this is objectionable for skaters in the vicinity of cities and towns;

A Treatise on Skating

because, on backward movements, *if rounded*, they will *run upon* chips, nutshells, scraps and fragments of all sorts dropped by the crowds, and so cause falls and stumbles: whereas the *rectangular* termination under the heel will *turn aside* such matters.

There should be no hook, nor the germ of a hook, at the toe. A scrolled or turned-up iron at the toe, may, if properly formed, be ornamental, but is of no use, and, amongst skaters is dangerous in case of falls. In Edinburgh, two gentlemen ran violently against each other, and fell: One had his face shockingly torn by the hook or turn-up of the skate of his friend, which disfigured him for life. The *curve* of the *iron*, as well as its *depth* from the sole of the foot to its lower edge, will depend upon the *skater*, and his style of action, as well as upon the *breadth* of the *sole* of his *foot*. A *bold* impetuous *skater* should have but *a slight curve* to the iron. One who prefers figuring in *a small space* and on crowded ice, requires *more curve*, to enable him to make *shorter turns*. The *curve*, therefore, should vary from that of the segment of a circle of two feet radius, to one of nine feet.[59] The *depth* of the *iron*, from the sole of the boot or shoe, should, in accordance with the foregoing remarks, be, including the stock, from $1\frac{3}{8}$ to $1\frac{7}{8}$ inches. The more dexterous the skater, the deeper should be his iron, to prevent the edge of the sole of his boot or shoe, in the act of making extreme inclinations and sudden turns, from touching the ice, and so causing the iron to slip from under the foot, and bring him violently down. The *thickness* of the *iron* at the lower edges may be from $\frac{1}{8}$ of an inch full, to $\frac{1}{4}$ of an inch, according to fancy. Irons of skates, expressly for running swiftly forwards, should be deeper under the heel than under the toe; or, if not so formed, in racing, the heel of the skater should be raised on the stock by an additional ply of leather to the heel of his boot or shoe.

The *Stock and Fastenings* of skates are of various forms and methods. Some skaters have the stocks screwed, or otherwise fastened, to their boots or shoes, Some, again, have a piece of plate-iron fixed across the stock at the heel, and a piece of the same sort on the tread; these pieces have their ends turned up, to fit over the edges of the heel and sole: others have only one of these plates, according to fancy: This plan, when there is not considerable depth of iron, is dangerous; because, upon any extraordinary inclination of the body, the iron which projects beyond the edges of the sole or heel, may touch the ice, and throw the skate off its edge, and so cause a violent fall: an improvement is, however, made, by sinking the turned-up ends of the plates into the edges of the leather. Some skates have a spring plate under the heel, screwed or fastened to the stock at that part under the instep, with a pike near the extremity to run into the heel of the boot: this is *Savigny's Patent*.[60] The excellence of which is, that it gives to the heel the fullest play vertically, which is essential, while it secures against any change of position on the stock horizontally. A similar kind of spring is sometimes fixed in front, towards or under the toe, with sharp iron points on it, which sink into the sole by the pressure of the body, and so fixes the forefoot, and gives play to the toe.

A stock, nearly the breadth of the foot, with springs affixed,—of the kind now mentioned, and one, two, or three iron points on the tread, to sink into the sole of the boot; *with an iron as before described and recommended; with a short broad strap to buckle over the instep, and a long strap in front, properly adjusted* to pass before and behind the ball of the great toe; and to buckle, forming a St. Andrew's cross on top, or, instead of the latter strap, *Savigny's Sliding Toe-springs* (or plates), which *grip the sole* of a boot of *any* width, and buckle on top of the *forefoot*, and thus *fasten it and the stock together* at such parts of each as may be most agreeable to the foot of the skater—as a whole, *will form a skate*, to the construction of which, very *few can find any material objection*. The stock of any skate may be widened by sinking into it, and screwing down, a brass plate across the tread.

Sir William Newton, the President of the London Skating Club, is of opinion that the method adopted by Mr. *Priest* of Oxford Street, of *fastening* the skate to the *heel* of the boot, is the best; and assigns, as one reason, that there should be no play at the heel. An instep strap is all that is required, provided the fore-foot be secured to the skate by a cramp (to be immediately described), as above mentioned.

Some have the skate and a *laced* boot fastened together by screws, rivets, &c., without any straps, which is an excellent and comfortable plan. Some skates have the fore part of the wooden stock curved upwards, to correspond with the curve of the sole of the boot, with sharp iron points on it to sink into the leather. *Mr.*

Coleman, Haymarket, adapts a *cramp*, screwed to the fore part of the stock, which grips the sole of the boot before the tread by doubling over the upper edge of the leather: a fore-strap is thus entirely dispensed with.[61]

"*Rogers's Patent Skate*," is a laudable endeavour: its slight imprefections in *forms*, are apparent to a skater. The *conception, as a whole, with practical modifications*, claims precedence.[62]

Lieutenant Jones describes his favourite method of fastening on skates as follows:—"Let the skates be prepared with heel and toe straps, as usual; but, instead of heel pegs, let the heel-screws be made with flat heads, and long enough to go through the heels of the shoes, in which holes must be bored, and the heads of the screws sunk even with the leather, to prevent hurting the feet; to guard against which more effectually, let a piece of leather be sewed to the quarter of the shoe, large enough to cover the whole heel, which will defend it sufficiently from the screw. This method has the following advantages:—Firstly, by the screw going through the lifts of the heel, the skate is prevented from altering its position in that part; secondly, when this sort of heel screw is used, the straps are not required to be drawn so tight as to give pain to the feet. An objection may, upon good grounds, be made to fastening the shoe to the skate without straps, because the skates have thereby no proper play. But this method of screwing them at the heel had by no means the same bad effect; for the screws being in the centre, and the leather pliable, the shoes have their liberty at the sides. Experience has taught me that the skate must not be confined at the toes; and yet it is necessary to prevent it there also from slipping. The points of iron on the tread are continued for that purpose."

Ladies' Skates should be fluted:[63] the fastenings, either straps and buckles, or laced—over the fore-foot and instep.

Further remarks upon irons, stocks, and fastenings, would be of but little use: These may vary with the physical constitution, taste, and experience of the skater. It would advance our science rapidly, if skate-makers and skate vendors were, more frequently than they are, skaters also.

To proceed to action:—

Travelling backwards

This is a substantial revision of the section on skating backwards in the 1772 edition (page 78).

On the inside edge. To make a stroke on the left leg; turn in the toe of the right foot, and press the inside edge of it towards the point, which will force you backwards upon the left leg: lean forward as much as you can during the movement: the same method must be followed for the other leg, reversing the motion. A good deal of practice is required. When proficient in forcing yourself backwards upon the inside edge, you may make *bold* inside-edge circular *sweeps with* the *propelling leg*, which will *send you* insensibly round *backwards upon* the *outside edge* of the other leg. This latter movement, when acquired, will be found very agreeable and refreshing.

Outside wheel and outside edge backwards

This section and figure 17 were added after Jones's description of a figure of a heart (page 78), in the 1855 edition.

We come now to a difficult, and at the same time one of the most agreeable manœuvres. It would seem to be difficult, from the circumstance that so few skaters attempt to perform it. A bold skater has, however, only to try, to succeed. This movement brings round a refreshing change from the monotonous inside turn and inside edge-backward scroll. It is performed this:—Try with the right leg first:—*Strike out*, gently at first, upon the right leg, *squaring the toe well out*, as in the fencing position, and at the same time giving the body a latent impetus of "right shoulder forward:" this impetus will soon wheel the body quickly round to the outside edge backward. Try again, and again, observing these directions, and it will be soon acquired. Having become proficient on the right, try the left leg; observing, when striking out upon it, to *square the toe well out*, giving, at the same instant an impetus to the body of "left shoulder forward." The more you square out the toe at striking off, the longer you will continue on the leg before the impetus with which you started will bring you round; and the longer you can defer the wheel-about, the quicker it will be made, and the more agreeable becomes the movement to the skater.

Serpentine line backwards

This section was added after the outside wheel section in the 1855 edition.

When[64] master of the foregoing manœuvre, it will be found to be by far the easiest and best under which to perform a Serpentine Line Backwards; and from which, also, the skater can run into various other figures with a greater flow of ease than from any other.

Concluding injunction

This section is an expansion of the last sentence of the 1772 edition. It remains at the end of the book, after Cormack's description of the outside wheel.

There are various other movements performed on skates besides those treated of.

But the skater who can perform all those manœuvres mentioned, and flow through the whole of them, in that order which may be the easiest of succession to himself, will require no further instructions to invent and vary.

Let the skater always bear in mind to *keep up* his *impetus*, so as to involve anticipation of running into other and different movements. And also, that the *changes* of

Figure 17: The outside wheel and outside edge backwards (1855).

position, and of *inclination* of the *head, arms,* and *legs,* &c. *reversely* and *inversely,* as demanded, *to poize* the whole *person, relatively to the* intended *movements,* forwards and retrograde, &c. upon the inside and outside edges, &c. *constitute the key to the* perfect and easy *performance* of all the graceful and difficult manœuvres and evolutions.

Commentary

Notes

1. The quote that opens the book is from the poem "Winter" in the 1744 version of *The Seasons* by James Thomson (1700–1748).

2. Several bone skates have been found at Moorfields. The earliest published example is the skate shown in figure C1, which was described by Charles Roach Smith and Alfred Smee in "Bone Skate Found at Moorfield," *Archæologia, or Miscellaneous Tracts Relating to Antiquity* 29 (1842): 397–399; a drawing is printed in the former's *Collectanea Antiqua: Etchings and Notices of Ancient Remains Illustrative of the Habits, Customs, and History of Past Ages* (London: J. R. Smith, 1848).

Figure C1: Drawing of a bone skate found at Moorfields, London. From Charles Roach Smith, *Collectanea Antiqua: Etchings and Notices of Ancient Remains Illustrative of the Habits, Customs, and History of Past Ages* (London: J. R. Smith, 1848), 167.

3. This is almost a direct quote from an anonymous eighteenth-century translation published as "A description of the most honourable city of London, written originally in Latin by William Fitzstephen, a monk of Canterbury, who flourished in the reign of Henry II," in *The Annual Register, or a View of the History, Politicks, and Literature for the Year 1764* (London: J. Dodsley, 1765), 182–183. I have corrected the most obvious errors in transcription (Jones had *skates* for *stakes* twice), but left others (*flick* for *strike* and *heads* for *head*).

4. Tasso actually lived in the sixteenth century, from 1544 to 1595, according to Douglas B. Killings, "Gerusalemme liberata ("Jerusalem delivered") by Torquato Tasso (1544–1595)," in *The Online Medieval and Classical Library*, vol. 14 (1995).

5. This is the beginning of verse 34 of book or canto 14 of Torquato Tasso's *Gerusalemme liberata* (Jerusalem delivered), which was first published in 1581. Edward Fairfax translated it as follows:

> As on the Rhene, when winter's freezing cold
> Congeals the streams to thick and hardened glass,
> The beauties fair of shepherds' daughters bold
> With wanton windlaws run, turn, play and pass.

This translation was first published in England in 1600

and formed the basis of Henry Morley's 1901 edition before being published in *The Online Medieval and Classical Library*.

6. This seems to be a reference to William Cadogan, *A Dissertation on the Gout, and All Chronic Diseases, Jointly Considered, as Proceeding from the Same Causes; What Those Causes Are; and a Rational and Natural Method of Cure Proposed* (London: J. Dodsley, 1771).

7. The first three editions had "thread" with an erratum correcting it to "tread." The correction was finally made in the 1797 edition.

8. The blades were rockered, like modern figure skates. This means that the blade is curved from end to end so that the skater balances on a short part of it at a time. H. E. Vandervell (*The Figure Skate: A Research into the Form of Blade Best Adapted to Curvilinear Skating*, 24) argued that the ideal rocker radius is 9 feet for combined skating and 3 feet for small figures, like loops, with 6 feet as a happy medium. Modern figure skates typically have a radius of curvature of seven or eight feet. For a full discussion of rockering as it applies to Jones's skates, see page 155.

9. The rest of this section is omitted in the 1823 edition.

10. The blades were tapered.

11. This probably refers to the type of sharpening that is done with modern figure and hockey skates. The bot-

tom of the blade is ground so that its cross section is concave. The radius of curvature, called the radius of hollow, is typically close to one-half inch for freestyle and hockey; skates used for figures (patch skates) generally have a radius of hollow of at least one inch.

12. The errata included a change from "shall dispense" to "may be dispensed," which has been dispensed with here. The 1797 edition did not incorporate this erratum either.

13. This paragraph was merged into the next in the 1855 edition.

14. The 1823 edition changed "also" to "always".

15. In the 1855 edition, the previous paragraph was inserted here, and "As a general rule, incline,—first the eyes and head, next the shoulders, then the arms,—the body, the legs, and the skate, in succession, towards whichever side you wish to go." was added.

16. The word "young" was removed in the 1855 edition.

17. Again, "young" was removed in the 1855 edition.

18. This phrase was changed to "as sometimes proves hurtful" in the 1855 edition.

19. The 1855 edition adds the a note here: "Previously

to going on the ice, the learner should practice both walking about with his skates on, and balancing himself on either foot on a wooden floor."

20. This word was changed to "point" in the 1855 edition.

21. The 1823 and subsequent editions ended this paragraph here and omitted the following explanation and figures.

22. This word was corrected to "because" in the 1797 edition.

23. The 1823 edition resumed here.

24. In the 1855 edition, the first two paragraphs were replaced with "We come to a movement, which appears very agreeable to the eye, and which all beginners are ambitious of attaining."

25. In the 1855 edition, this paragraph was changed to "To preserve the balance on the outside edge, requires more skill than any of the former positions; it is difficult to be acquired, but will be easier in practice than it appears in theory. Many spend three or four winters in learning it. But this is to be imputed principally to their not having pursued a proper method at first setting out."

26. The 1855 edition added "The *cross outside edge* is done by passing one leg across the other in front, and striking out with the foot as it comes down on the ice."

27. This clause was deleted in the 1855 edition.

28. Rolling is caricatured by the first skater on the second row of Cruikshank's engraving from *Eccentric Excursions* (page 21). Figures 7 and 8 replaced this figure in later editions. The 1823 version of this figure figure is sometimes identified as a picture of Robert Jones himself; that seems unlikely because the *Times* had reported his death in 1788. If he was still alive, he would have been in his eighties.

29. This section was retitled "The great inside circle, or spread eagle" and figure 9 was added in the 1855 edition. It must have been fairly popular before then, because it is shown in the upper left of Cruikshank's engraving (page 21) despite the absence of a drawing in the earlier editions of Jones's book.

30. Before "on," "—right shoulder forward—" was added in the 1855 edition.

31. This clause was changed to "so that they poize the body" in the 1855 edition.

32. In the 1865 edition, "off your" was changed to "him off his".

33. In the 1855 edition, "is difficult, and" was removed.

34. The flying Mercury seems to have been very popular; the central column of Cruikshank's engraving (page 21) shows two different views of a man performing it.

35. In the earliest editions, the figures showing the flying Mercury and the fencing position were swapped. This is corrected in this edition. Figures 11 and 12 replaced the flying Mercury drawing in later editions.

36. This phrase was replaced with "about the middle of the stroke" in 1855.

37. This section was retitled "The fencing attitude" in the 1855 edition.

38. Cormack added "as in spread eagle" in the 1855 edition.

39. The original has "...in the fourth Plate", but the fourth plate in that edition showed the flying Mercury. The fencing position was in the third plate. Figure 14 replaced figure 13 in the 1823 and 1825 editions. In the 1855 edition, this sentence was removed and figure 15 replaced figure 13.

40. "There are other forms of salutation" was added in the 1855 edition.

41. In the 1855 edition, "or spread eagle" was added.

42. This sentence was not included in the 1855 edition.

43. This section was substantially revised and expanded in the 1855 edition. See page 113.

44. The 1823 edition begins this section "This is a pleasing manœuvre, if well done."

45. The 1855 edition starts this section here.

46. This sentence was moved to the "Concluding injunction" (page 115) in the 1855 edition.

47. Changed to "THE END." in 1825.

48. Cyclos (George Anderson) adds a few notes about this skate in the first (1852) edition of his book:

> Boot skates I have never used, but have heard them well spoken of. For ladies, I should consider them by far the best description. The skate iron is just inserted in the thick sole of a lacing ancle boot, and there is no fastening, beyond putting on the boot, and lacing it firmly. It is no new invention, and I therefore think if there was not some strong objection, it would have found more general favour with skaters. I find it advertised upwards of sixty years ago, as
>
> *"The new invented half-boot skait, sold by the inventor, Mr. James, No. 14, Newgate Street, and by Thomas Olio Rickman, No. 7, Upper Mary-le-bone Street. Price one guinea and a-half."*
>
> So, it has had at least plenty of time to introduce itself. One objection is, that in-

stead of only a pair of skates, you have to carry a pair of boots to the ice, and may have some difficulty in the disposal, while there, of the walking boots you take off.

Cyclos dates the introduction of these skates to the early 1790s, which conflicts with T.C.R.'s note that half-boot skates were "here offered to the public for the first time" in 1797. Since Cyclos quotes the advertisement on page 92 precisely, this is probably what he was referring to, and the skates were introduced 55 years before he he wrote.

49. This is probably T. C. Rickman, the bookseller.

50. This is probably a typo for "Clio."

51. The rest of the new section is nearly the same as the section on skating in Sholto Percy and Reuben Percy, *The Percy Anecdotes: Anecdotes of Pastime* (London: T. Boys, 1821), 62–64.

52. This was reported in the article on skating written by a member of the Edinburgh Skating Club and published in the appendix to the second edition of the *Encyclopedia Britannica* (1783).

53. This quotation is from Joseph Strutt, *Gil-Gamena Angel-deod. Or, the Sports and Pastimes of the People of England* (London: T. Bensley, 1801), 69.

54. The closing quotation mark is missing in the 1823 edition.

55. This was John Gittam of Nordelph. In 1823, William Ayres of Earith beat him by skating half a mile in one minute, according to a wooden board quoted by Enid Porter ("Fen Skating," 51). In their *Handbook of Fen Skating* (London: Sampson, Low, Marston, Searle, and Rivington, 1882), Neville and Albert Goodman provide details of the races and records in early fen skating and suggest that Gittam wasn't actually that fast:

> It will be found that, whenever any man ran against time for a wager (i.e.) whenever there was anyone strongly interested in seeing that the time and distance were accurately taken, the time in which one mile was done was never less than 3min, and often considerably more. (Goodman and Goodman, 55)

56. The Flying Childers (1715–1741) was "the fleetest horse that ever ran at Newmarket, or, as generally believed, that was ever bred in the world," according to Whyte (*History of the British Turf*, I.424–425).

57. Jones would have been about 115 years old in 1855.

58. "Recent" was changed to "late" in the 1865 edition. Cormack's recommended skates are similar to the most popular ones described (but not recommended) by Van-

dervell and Witham (*A System of Figure-Skating, Being the Theory and Practice of the Art as Developed in England, with a Glance at Its Origin and History*, 65):

> The skate most generally in use is made after this fashion: a wooden bed, hollowed out to fit the boot as closely as possible; three small spikes in the front part of it to enter the sole, and a good screw or pike to go into the heel; the iron of the skate extending but a trifle beyond the length of the foot, and rounded fore and aft.

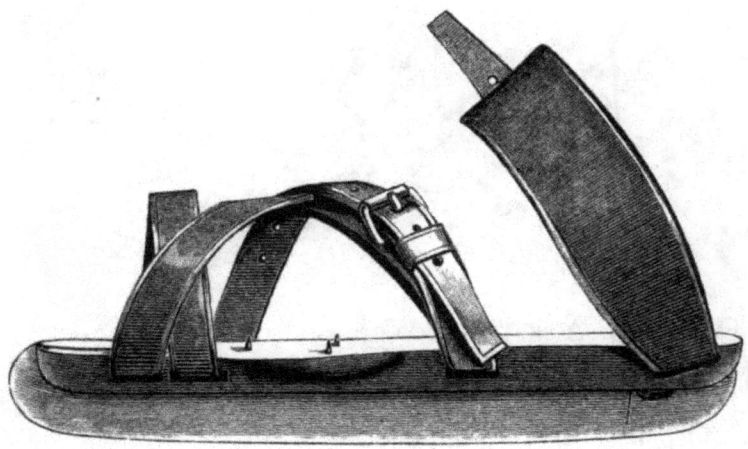

Figure C2: The most popular type of skate described by Vandervell and Witham (1869).

59. Today a radius of curvature (rocker radius) of seven or eight feet is the norm for figure skates.

60. John Horatio Savigny patented his skate design on December 4, 1784. The UK patent number is 1458, according to the list in Bennet Woodcroft, *Alphabetical Index of Patentees of Inventions*, first published in 1854 (London: Evelyn, Adams, & MacKay, 1969), 502.

61. See figure C3 for a drawing of a skate with a cramp.

Figure C3: A skate with a cramp from H. E. Vandervell and T. Maxwell Witham, *A System of Figure-Skating, Being the Theory and Practice of the Art as Developed in England, with a Glance at Its Origin and History* (London: Macmillan & Company, 1869), 68.

62. Rodgers's patent skate has been discussed in *Kouwe Drukte* (see Anrie Broere, "Een vroege klapschaats," *Kouwe Drukte* 2, no. 6 (September 1999): 15–16 and

Niko Mulder, "Patent ontwerp — een vroege klapschaats? (2)," *Kouwe Drukte* 3, no. 7 (December 1999): 5). To summarize, patent number 6062 was granted to George Rodgers on January 18, 1831 (Woodcroft, *Alphabetical Index of Patentees of Inventions*, 487). The design was very popular but not universally acclaimed. Cyclos (*The Art of Skating with Plain Directions for the Acquirement of the Most Difficult and Elegant Maneuvers*, 30) remarks,

> I used this skate for some years, but considered it insecure. The iron has too little support, and vibrates while skating, to such a degree that I have known it break; and being, for the sake of strength, of a uniform thickness, the edge does not catch the ice so well as those irons which are thinner at the foot than at the ice. It is also, like the common skate, too long at the toe and too short at the heel.
>
> I do not think, however, that many of the objections I have named, might be obviated in construction, so that this beautiful skate might become thoroughly practical, which it is not at present. The price, I think runs from 20s. to 25s.

Vandervell (*The Figure Skate: A Research into the Form of Blade Best Adapted to Curvilinear Skating*, 13–14) considered the skate unsafe:

> The safety of the skate was dependent on the spring. There was a terrible strain upon

it in certain positions, springs broke and skaters were injured, and the skate was only used when the heel strap was tightened up, to bring the spring foot plate right down permanently, so that the sole use of the spring then was to keep the peg in the heel.

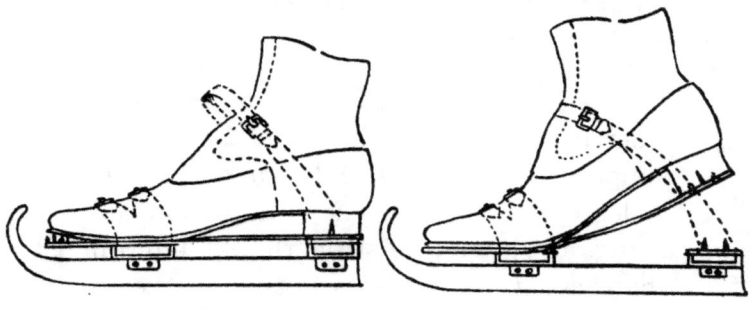

Figure C4: Rodgers' patent skate. Drawing from H. E. Vandervell, *The Figure Skate: A Research into the Form of Blade Best Adapted to Curvilinear Skating* (London: Straker Brothers, 1901), 14.

63. Compare Jones's original advice on page 43.

64. This section was added in the 1855 edition.

Editions of the *Treatise*

This chapter presents an annotated list of all the previous editions of Robert Jones's *Treatise*, with and without additions and emendations.* It is complete as far as I know, though there is always the possibility that more editions will surface. The availability of the various editions at the time of writing is summarized in table 1.

Information on these editions is primarily drawn from various library catalogs† and two articles:

- Nigel Brown, "Skating: 'a very pretty art'," *The Book Collector* 25, no. 6 (1977): 537–565

- Fred. W. Foster, *A Bibliography of Skating* (London: B. W. Warhurst, 1898)

I've followed the library catalogs (mainly the British Library) in assigning dates to the editions without dates printed on the title page. Some of these dates may be inaccurate, and I've explained in those sections.

---

*This chapter was originally published, in a slightly different form, under the title "1772 Robert Jones, A Treatise on Skating" on *Schaatshistorie.nl*.

†Particularly the British Library, the Bodleian Library at Oxford University, the Cambridge University Library, and OCLC WorldCat.

Edition	Bodleian	CUL	BL	Google Books	ECCO	Foster	Brown
1772	No?	No	Yes	—	CW0103542877	Yes	Yes
1775?	No?	No	Yes	IyZhAAAAcAAJ	—	No	Yes
1780?	Yes?	No	Yes	ObdwnXxrDTkC	CW0102363611	Yes	Yes
1797	No	No	No	kh4FSQAACAAJ*	CW0103106130	No	Yes
1818	No	Yes	No	—	—	Yes	No
1823	No	No	Yes	6_tAqlopPiwC	—	No	Yes
1825?	Yes	No	Yes	MQ8dCAOod3EC	—	No	No
1855?	Yes	Yes	Yes	9EECAAAAQAAJ	—	Yes	No
1865?	No	No	No	—	—	Yes	Yes
2017	No	No	No	dPDKswEACAAJ*	—	No	No
2023	No	No	No	fK6qzwEACAAJ*	—	No	No

Table 1: Availability of the various editions. CUL = Cambridge University Library; BL = British Library. The identification codes for Google Books and Gale Eighteenth-Century Collections Online (ECCO) are listed when available. A superscripted asterisk means that no preview is available. For the Bodleian items with question marks, see the notes under the 1780 edition.

Under the original title

Full title: *A Treatise on Skating; founded on certain Principles deduced from many Years' experience; by which that noble Exercise is now reduced to an Art, and may be taught and learned by a regular Method, with both Ease and Safety. The Whole illustrated with Copper-plates, representing the Attitudes and Graces.*

There are five known editions under the original title (with some spelling variation).

1772

First edition, xvi+64 pages, 4 plates, octavo (129×212 mm). Printed for the author and sold by J. Ridley in St. James's Street, London.

No price is listed on the title page. The *Critical Review*[*] sets it at one shilling sixpence, but Foster[†] and a later issue of the catalogue in the *Monthly Review*[‡] report it as two shillings sixpence. Page xii is misnumbered as xiv, and page 62 is misnumbered as 60.

This edition includes a dedication to Lord Spencer Hamilton and a preface that puts skating in historical context and encourages women to participate. The original edition is illustrated by two anonymous line drawings depicting journeys plus four copper-plate en-

---

[*] "Monthly catalogue," item 54, p. 184.

[†] Foster, *A Bibliography of Skating*, 31.

[‡] "Monthly catalogue, for May, 1772," *The Monthly Review; or, Literary Journal* 46 (1772): item 37, p. 543.

gravings by William Darling: two views of an English skate plus three skating maneuvers (common rolling, the flying Mercury, and the fencing position).

Hines[*] claims that the book was printed twice in 1772, and Foster[†] does list two printings in 1772, but the second is actually the edition commonly dated to 1780. It does seem possible that a second 1772 printing could have been required if the book was originally published in January or February (consistent with its appearance in the February 1772 edition of the *Critical Review*'s "Monthly Catalogue"[‡]) and demand for it increased substantially in the summer due to media coverage of Jones's trial. Norton[§] says the book "was published during the course of his trial" without citing any evidence. The price change in the May catalog may perhaps be evidence of a reprint, but if so, it was not linked to Jones's trial, which took place in July. It may also be that the *Monthly Review* was slower to pick up the book than the *Critical Review*.

Gale ECCO (Eighteenth-Century Collections Online) has reprinted the copy in the British Library under the ISBNs 978-1-170-36434-5 (paperback, 2010) and 978-1-379-92300-8 (hardcover, 2018).

---

[*]James R. Hines, *Figure Skating in the Formative Years: Singles, Pairs, and the Expanding Role of Women* (Urbana: University of Illinois Press, 2015), 6n3.

[†]Foster, *A Bibliography of Skating*, 31.

[‡]"Monthly catalogue," item 54, p. 184.

[§]Norton, "Jones, Captain Robert."

1775?

Reprint of the first edition, iv+64 pages, 4 plates, octavo. Printed for the author and sold by C. Fourdrinier, Charing Cross "and all other Booksellers and News Carriers."

This edition is attributed to "a gentleman" rather than Jones by name. No date is given on the title page; the British Library has inferred 1775. The title page includes a place for a price, but none is visible in the British Library's copy. Another copy gives the price as one shilling sixpence.

The dedication and preface are missing, and the note that skates may be purchased at Riccard's Manufactory is pasted in. The engraving showing the skates is at the back of the book, with the other engravings, instead of in the text. The British Library's copy has a handwritten note on library stationary tipped-in that says:

> Compared with Robert Jones' edition of 1772 (supposed to be the first), it appears 1. that sheets B to E were from the type of 1772, and had not been reset. The same misprints occur in both: e.g.
> > p. 25, line penult edgc
> > . 29, line 2 perfomed
> > . 30, line antepenult. bacause
> > . 62 printed as p. 60
>
> The only correction which I have found is that the 1772 edition heads p. 62 "A TREAT", corrected in this copy by" [adding ISE in smaller letters.]

I was not able to view the rest of the note, but did manage to puzzle out some of the text on the back by looking at what showed through. It appears to add that the plates had been moved to the end of the book and that sheet A of the 1772 edition had been replaced. The note's writer speculates that these changes—especially the replacement of Jones's name—could have been made to conceal the author's identity in response to Jones's trial.

Brown* suggested that this printing (and the next) were pirated. While many stories are improved by the addition of pirates and they cannot be ruled out here, I think a more straightforward explanation suffices. Sheet A was lost, a few corrections were made, and Jones's name was removed because he was unpopular due to his conviction and exile. With this explanation, the title page's statement that the book was "printed for the author" could even be correct—Jones could have asked for it to be printed from abroad. The weakness of this explanation becomes apparent with the next edition.

1780?

Reprint of the first edition labeled as the second edition, xvi+64 pages, 4 plates, octavo. Printed for the author and sold by J. Williams, 39 Fleet Street; C. Fourdrinier, Charing Cross; and T. Jones, Clare Court, Drury Lane.

This edition appears identical to the 1772 edition except for the title page. The heading on p. 62, which

---

*Brown, "Skating: 'a very pretty art'," 540.

was corrected in the 1775 edition, is not corrected in this edition, and pages xii and 62 are misnumbered. The title page adds "the second edition" and the price (two shillings), but has no date.

This edition complicates the explanation for the previous edition that I put forward because sheet A had returned and the errors that were corrected had been uncorrected. This makes sense if the putative 1780 edition was actually published before the putative 1775 edition, which is possible: Foster* and the Bodleian Library both dated it to 1772 (with the Bodleian adding a question mark), and Brown[†] speculated that the 1775 and 1780 editions were actually printed in reverse order (1780 first) because of the changes in the 1775 edition. It is possible that this was the second 1772 printing mentioned by Foster and above, under "1772."

The British Library's copy includes the sheet music for "The Skaiter's March," which the catalog notes has been "extracted from the July 1782 issue of the 'European Magazine'." This could have been added by the book's owner years after it was published.

Gale ECCO reprinted the copy in the British Library under the ISBNs 978-1-170-35776-7 (paperback, 2010) and 978-1-379-91657-4 (hardcover, 2018).

---

*Foster, *A Bibliography of Skating*, 31.
[†]Brown, "Skating: 'a very pretty art'," 540.

1797

Revised version published under the slightly different title *A Treatise on Skaiting*, viii+52 pages, 4 plates, octavo. Printed for J. Walker, 44 Pater-Noster-Row; and T. C. Rickman, 7 Upper Mary-Le-Bone Street.

This edition includes a new foreword by "T. C. R." (presumably T. C. Rickman, the printer) noting that the book has been lightly revised and advertising "the new invented Half-Boot Skait", which attaches directly to the skater's boot at both toe and heel without a wooden base. The original preface and dedication were removed. The main contents and plates have only minor changes such as the correction of errata and changes in spelling, most notably "skate" to "skait".

Gale ECCO reprinted the copy in the British Library under the ISBNs 978-1-170-35829-0 (paperback, 2010) and 978-1-379-91709-0 (hardcover, 2018).

1818

Reprint of the 1797 edition under the title *A Treatise on Skaiting* with the designation "a new edition" on the title page. viii+52 pages, 21 cm. Printed for J. Arnould, 2 Spring Gardens.

This appears to be a reprint of the 1797 edition. The final sentence of the title ("The whole illustrated with Copper-plates, representing the Attitudes and Graces") has been left off the title page, but the foreword by

T. C. R. from the 1797 edition is included in place of the original preface and dedication. The plates are the same as in previous editions.

The only surviving library copy appears to be the one at Cambridge University.

Under the revised title

Full title: *The Art of Skating; founded on certain principles deduced from many years' experience; by which That noble, healthy, and agreeable Exercise, is reduced to an Art, and may be taught and learned by a regular method, with ease and safety. Illustrated with plates, representing the attitudes and graces.*

There are four known editions under this title. Two were published in the 1820s with essentially the same content as the eighteenth-century editions but the plates replaced by a single color fold-out plate. The other two were substantially revised by William Eppes Cormack and include new black-and-white line drawings.

1823

First edition under the new title, vi+24 pages, 1 fold-out plate, duodecimo. Printed and sold for the author by Y. G. Smeeton, 15 Royal Arcade, Pall Mall.

The eighteenth-century copper plates were replaced with a single new color fold-out drawing of a man in a top hat performing the three moves of the original. The original dedication was replaced with a revised preface that reprinted on page 93.

The general contents of the book are the same. Two sections have been cut: Jones's details of the construction of skates (pages 42–45) and the discussion of traveling along "a channel or road" from "Suppose a journey of ten miles..." on page 51 to "the most trifling proposition" on page 53.

The British Library's catalog entry lists William Eppes Cormack as a contributor. While there is no direct evidence for this in the text, the new title and the revisions that foreshadow the 1855 edition, which Cormack clearly was responsible for, suggest that he may have been involved. Nigel Brown* took the statement on the title page that the book was "printed and sold for the author" as evidence that Jones was still alive to do the revisions, but this conflicts with the *Times*'s report of his death in 1788 (page 16).

1825

Reprint of the 1823 edition, vi+24 pages, 1 fold-out plate, duodecimo. Printed for William Cole, 10 Newgate Street, by G. H. Davidson, Ireland Yard, Doctors' Commons.

No date is given on the title page; the British Library has inferred 1825. This edition begins with a "Preface to the first edition" that is the 1823 preface and includes the figures from 1823. The 1825 version of the plate adds the caption "Published by Hodgson & Co. 10, Newgate."

---

*Brown, "Skating: 'a very pretty art'," 545.

The text is the same as the 1823 edition, but minor variations in punctuation, capitalization, and layout show that it has been reset (e.g., the sentence beginning "N.B." has been moved from p. 24 to p. 23, and p. 24 ends with "THE END" instead of "FINIS").

The University of Connecticut has a copy of this book in its skating collection, but images are not available online. Based on emails with the staff, I have determined that it is the 1825 edition even though the catalog lists the date as 1805 as of this writing.

1855

New edition with additions and substantial revisions by William Eppes Cormack published under the shorter title *The Art of Skating, Practically Explained.* viii+40 pages, 5 plates, octavo (16 cm). Published by Baily Brothers, Printers, Stationers and General Advertising Agents, 3 Royal Exchange Buildings, Cornhill.

The date is not printed on the title page, but the Bodleian Library has inferred 1855. The "preface to the first edition" in this volume is a lightly revised version of the 1823 preface (page 99). A new "preface to the present edition" was added (page 105) that includes remarks that Jones "may be laid up with gout" and "that he has not heard the loud calls, in 1852, for his Treatise." It is possible that these calls were related to the publication of George Anderson's *The Art of Skating* under the pseudonym "Cyclos" (see page 22). The title page sets the price at one shilling.

The plates are entirely new and designated "from a

tablotype by Henneman & Malone" and "J. Brandard lith." They depict five maneuvers: rolling, the great inside circle or spread eagle, the flying Mercury, the fencing attitude, and the outside wheel and outside edge backwards.

HardPress reprinted the copy in the Bodleian Library under the ISBN 978-1-318-68758-9 (2019, paperback).

1865

Reprint of the 1855 edition. viii+40 pages, 5 plates, octavo (17 cm). Published by Baily Brothers, 3 Royal Exchange Buildings.

The title page includes neither date nor author details. It is a reprint of the 1855 edition that has been reset with some minor changes, mainly to punctuation and occasionally to capitalization. The artists' credits on the plates have been removed. Foster sets the price at 1 shilling.

This edition is elusive; the only library I've found that lists the actual book in its catalog is the Zentralbibiothek der Sportwissenschaften der deutschen Sporthochschule Köln. Memorial University in Newfoundland has a bound photocopy, and the New York Public Library has a microfilm copy. The New York copy was donated by A. G. Spalding's widow in 1921 as part of a large collection of sports memorabilia, mostly relating to baseball. Jones's book and a few others on skating are included in the collection's catalog.* The library now only has the microfilm copy, and the original was most likely destroyed after being filmed.

Recent

2017

A Treatise on Skating by R. Jones with contributions by W. E. Cormack, edited by B. A. Thurber. Evanston, IL: Skating History Press. iv+98 pages, 11 black and white figures, 127×203 mm, paperback. ISBN 978-1-948100-00-7.

The main text is from the 1772 edition; Cormack's additions are included as an appendix. The copper plates from the eighteenth-century editions and the line drawings from the 1855 edition are included. The sheet music bound with the British Library's copy of the 1780 edition has been reset. A new introduction and explanatory notes provide context. The 1823 and 1825 editions are not mentioned. This book has been superseded by the 2023 edition.

2023

This is the book you are reading now.

---

*New York Public Library, "The Spalding baseball collection," *Bulletin of the New York Public Library* 26, no. 1 (January 1922): 119.

Robert Jones's skates

London and Edinburgh

The skates Jones advises purchasing in the earlier editions of his book (page 40) are his own variation on late eighteenth-century skates. According to the note on page 36, they were sold at Riccard's Manufactory, which was rather like an eighteenth-century Wal-Mart. It sold all sorts of things, including dog collars, tweezers, knives, and medicine.* Compared with other skates of the time, Jones's skates are shorter and more curved to allow skaters to make tight turns. This meant they had to be taller, too. Jones also apparently made a number of smaller changes, which he details with his diagrams.

Examples of skates like the ones Jones recommends are hard to find. Even the skates in the figures Jones included in the first edition of his book (pages 60, 70, and 74) don't match his design. They look lower and flatter, with longer toes, rather like the skates in the chaotic *Skaiting Scene in Hyde Park* depicted in a 1785 etching held in the Lewis Walpole Library at Yale University. Those skates match the ones on the original emblem of the Edinburgh Skating Club.† The skates in the caricature from *Eccentric Excursions* (page 21) are

---

*Alun Withey, *Technology, Self-Fashioning and Politeness in Eighteenth-Century Britain* (New York: Palgrave Macmillan, 2016), 72.

†*The Edinburgh Skating-Club with Diagrams of Figures and*

even longer and flatter, and the skates in "Cold Broth and Calamity" (1792, figure C5) are curved like Jones's, but have large curls at the front.

The portraits of two Edinburgh Skating Club members painted in the late eighteenth century provide better information on the skates than the London caricatures because they were painted more for accuracy than for humor. William Grant, who had joined the club prior to 1778,[*] was painted by Gilbert Stewart in 1782.[†] This painting may have inspired the famous "Skating Minister" portrait of the Reverend Robert Walker from the 1790s currently held by the National Gallery of Scotland.[‡]

Unfortunately the details of the skates are hard to see in both paintings: Grant's in figure C6 and Walker's in figure C7. The blades have the general shape that Jones recommends, and it is possible to see straps crossing

---

a List of the Members (William Grant, 1865), 17–18. Several medals showing this emblem are in the National Museums of Scotland in Edinburgh; some can be viewed online.

[*] *The Edinburgh Skating-Club*, 6.

[†] The painting is called "The Skater" and now hangs in the National Gallery of Art in Washington, DC.

[‡] Walker had been admitted to the Edinburgh Skating Club in January, 1780, according to the list in *The Edinburgh Skating-Club*, 7. For a full discussion of this painting, see Duncan Thomson and Lynne Gladstone-Millar, *The Skating Minister: The Story behind the Painting* (Edinburgh: National Galleries of Scotland, 2004). An imaginative re-interpretation can be found in Michelle Sloan, *The Edinburgh Skating Club* (Edinburgh: Polygon Books, 2022).

A Treatise on Skating

Figure C5: Cold Broth and Calamity by Thomas Rowlandson (1792).

over his toes. Walker's skate has similar straps, but the heel is fastened by a clamp. While Grant's skates are clearly curved, Walker's look relatively flat.

Figure C6: William Grant's skates (1782).

Real-life skates like Jones's are even harder to find; I've come across only two examples so far. G. Herbert Fowler (1861–1940) had a copy of a similar skate from

A Treatise on Skating 153

Figure C7: Robert Walker's left foot (1790s).

around 1780 in his collection.* Sybolt Woudenberg got a pair of skates very like Walker's from a farmer in Groningen but was unable to find similar skates from the Netherlands and concluded that they may have been from Great Britain.† The blades are about 5 mm wide, which is slightly less than the quarter-inch Jones recommends at the heel (page 42). The curve at the front of the blade also looks longer than what Jones recommends.

All these skates have blades flatter than Jones's recommendation, which is consistent with what the *Encyclopædia Britannica* article cited from the 1823 edition onwards says:

> The English, though often remarkable for feats of agility upon skates, are very deficient in the article of grace; which is partly owing to the construction of the skates, which are too much curved in the surface which embraces the ice, consequently they involuntarily bring the users of them round on the outside upon a quick and small circle; whereas the skater, by using skates of a different construction, less curved, has the com-

---

*This skate is now in the London Science Museum, object number 1938-80.

†Sybolt Woudenberg, "Paar van de dominee?," *Kouwe Drukte* 17, no. 49 (December 2013): 6.

mand of his stroke, and can enlarge or diminish the circle according to his own wish and desire.*

Not surprisingly, this article was written by a member of the Edinburgh Skating Club "who has made the practice and improvement of skating his particular study."

Blade curvature

The extra curvature of the blade that the *Encyclopædia Britannica* disapproved of is a special feature of Jones's skates. Only a small part of the blade is in contact with the ice at any given time, which makes the blade less less stable but easier to maneuver. This is important for doing tricks like Jones's figure of a heart (called a three turn today).

Imagine the skate blade as part of a circle, as shown in figure C8.† The radius of that circle is called the rocker radius and is relatively simple to calculate by applying the Pythagorean Theorem to the triangle shown in figure C9. R is the radius of the circle, L is the distance from the point where the blade contacts the ice to the heel, and h is the distance from the ice to the heel of the blade.

---

*James Tytler, ed., *Encyclopædia Britannica*, second ed., vol. 10 (Edinburgh: J. Balfour & Co., et al., 1783), 9186.

†This refers to the main part of the blade. Skate blades almost always have more than one rocker radius because they curve upwards more sharply at the front and sometimes (e.g., in hockey skates) at the back.

Figure C8: The blade as part of a circle.

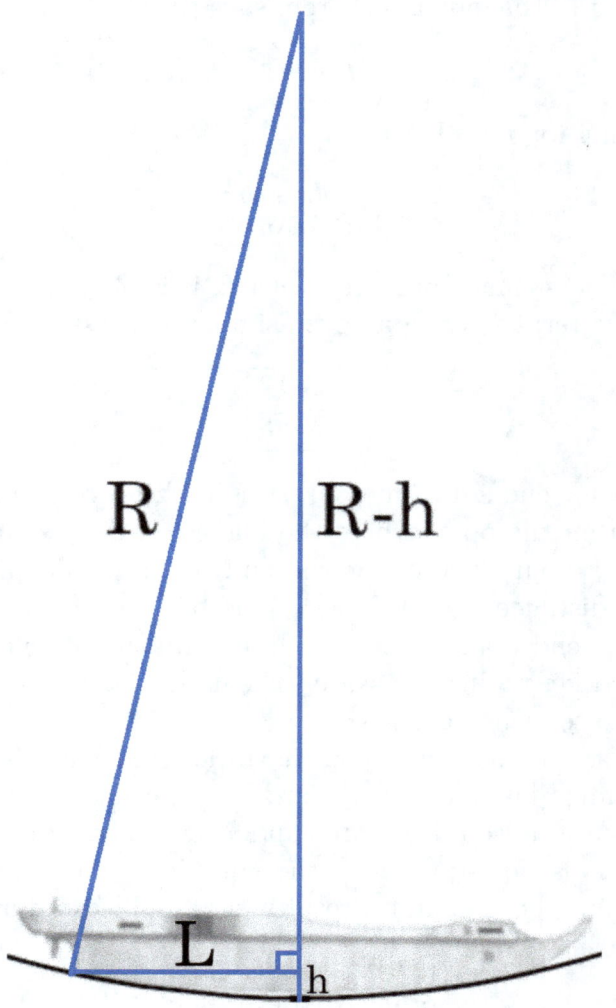

Figure C9: The triangle to use for calculating the rocker radius. The top vertex is the center of the circle.

The Pythagorean Theorem says that

$$L^2 + (R-h)^2 = R^2.$$

Solving for R yields

$$R = \frac{L^2 + h^2}{2h}.$$

Since h is small compared with L, it is okay to neglect the h^2 term,* giving an even simpler expression for R:

$$\boxed{R = \frac{L^2}{2h}}.$$

It's easy enough to measure L (the distance along the ice from the point where the blade touches its surface to the point just under the end of the blade) and h (the distance from the ice to the bottom of the blade at the end point). Plug in those numbers to calculate the rocker radius of a skate. The hardest part is getting accurate measurements.

Note that a small change in the length of the blade to accommodate a differently sized foot results in a flatter rocker because L is squared and, even though h changes too, it is not squared in the equation. For example, doubling both L and h results in a doubled radius:

$$R' = \frac{(2L)^2}{2(2h)} = \frac{4L^2}{4h} = \frac{L^2}{h} = 2R.$$

---

*Physicists make this kind of approximation all the time. If it bothers you, try calculating R using the formulas with and without h^2 and see how much they differ. Is that difference going to matter to the skater?

This would make a big difference to the skater! Jones does say that his skates are intended "for a middle-sized foot" and that the wooden footbed is $\frac{3}{4}$ of an inch thick. Using that as a scale for his diagram (figure 3 on page 44) and measuring accordingly results in a rocker radius of approximately four feet. For comparison, modern figure skate blades have 7- or 8-foot rockers, which are within the range (two to nine feet) recommended in the 1855 edition (p. 109) and consistent with H. E. Vandervell's recommendations: nine feet for combined skating, three feet for tight curves, and six feet as an all-around average.*

The description Jones starting on page 41 is clear and precise enough for a reader with some craft skills to make them. G. Herbert Fowler had a non-functional skate made of wood using Jones's pattern in his collection.† I also made a pair. I created the wooden footbed using modern power tools and had the blades laser cut from 1/4" mild steel based on a profile I created by blowing up Jones's diagram to match my foot size. I used the numbers Jones gave in the text for the height and width of the blade, but adjusted the length to fit my feet. I sharpened them so that they were flat across the bottom by draw-filing according to Hobart's instructions.‡

I calculated the rocker radius of my skates by measuring from the point where the blade balances on the

---

*Vandervell, *The Figure Skate: A Research into the Form of Blade Best Adapted to Curvilinear Skating*, 24.

†Fowler's replica skate is now in the London Science Museum, object number 1938-79.

‡James F. Hobart, "In a Clay County smith shop: An article

Figure C10: Robert Jones's skates reconstructed.

table to the end (12.8 cm) and the distance from the table to the heel of the blade (0.6 cm). This produced a rocker radius of about 1.37 m or close to 4.5 feet, just a little flatter than it looked like it should be from his diagram.

The most important difference between my skates and Jones's is that mine are not tapered; his are. Most of the tapering occurs at the prow of the skate, which does not touch the ice, so I don't think that difference affects their performance on the ice too much. I attached the skates to a pair of figure skating boots from the early 1990s and took to the ice. Their signficant curvature and flat cross-section made them very hard to skate on.

---

about a blacksmith who didn't want to do automobile repair work because it interfered with his regular business," *The Blacksmith and Wheelwright* 79, no. 3 (1919): 10–12.

Bibliography

Anonymous. "A description of the most honourable city of London, written originally in Latin by William Fitzstephen, a monk of Canterbury, who flourished in the reign of Henry II." In *The Annual Register, or a View of the History, Politicks, and Literature for the Year 1764*, 178–183. London: J. Dodsley, 1765.

Beer, E. S. de, ed. *The Diary of John Evelyn*. Oxford: Oxford University Press, 1959.

Blauw, Wiebe. *Van glis tot klapschaats: Schaatsen en schaatsenmakers in Nederland, 1200 tot heden*. Franeker: Van Wijnen, 2001.

Bright, Mynors, ed. *Diary and Correspondence of Samuel Pepys, Esp., F.R.S.: From His MS. Cypher in the Pepysian Library*. New York: Dodd, Mead, 1904.

Broere, Anrie. "Een vroege klapschaats." *Kouwe Drukte* 2, no. 6 (September 1999): 15–16.

Brown, Nigel. "Skating: 'a very pretty art'." *The Book Collector* 25, no. 6 (1977): 537–565.

Cadogan, William. *A Dissertation on the Gout, and All Chronic Diseases, Jointly Considered, as Proceeding from the Same Causes; What Those Causes Are; and a Rational and Natural Method of Cure Proposed*. London: J. Dodsley, 1771.

Carr, William. *Remarks of the Government of severall parts of Germanie, Denmark, Sweedland, Hamburg, Lubeck, and Hansiatique townes, but more particularly of the United Provinces.* Amsterdam: n.p., 1688.

Cormack, W. E. *Narrative of a Journey across the Island of Newfoundland in 1822.* St. John's, Newfoundland?: (n.p.), 1856.

Cyclos, John. *The Art of Skating with Plain Directions for the Acquirement of the Most Difficult and Elegant Maneuvers.* Glasgow: Thomas Murray & Son, 1852.

d'Avaux, Comte. *The Negotiations of Count d'Avaux.* London: A. Millar, D. Wilson, & T. Durham, 1754–1755.

The Edinburgh Skating-Club with Diagrams of Figures and a List of the Members. William Grant, 1865.

Foster, Fred. W. *A Bibliography of Skating.* London: B. W. Warhurst, 1898.

Goodman, Neville, and Albert Goodman. *Handbook of Fen Skating.* London: Sampson, Low, Marston, Searle, and Rivington, 1882.

Hines, James R. *Figure Skating in the Formative Years: Singles, Pairs, and the Expanding Role of Women.* Urbana: University of Illinois Press, 2015.

———. *Figure Skating: A History.* Urbana: University of Illinois Press, 2006.

"Historical Catalogue of the Exhibition of Skates, with Pictures and Other Matters Relating to Skating and Skaters, Held at the Hall of the Alpine Club, Feb. 10th to Feb. 15th, 1902." In *A History of the National Skating Association of Great Britain, 1879–1901*. London: National Skating Association, 1902.

Hobart, James F. "In a Clay County smith shop: An article about a blacksmith who didn't want to do automobile repair work because it interfered with his regular business." *The Blacksmith and Wheelwright* 79, no. 3 (1919): 10–12.

Killings, Douglas B. "Gerusalemme liberata ("Jerusalem delivered") by Torquato Tasso (1544–1595)." In *The Online Medieval and Classical Library*, vol. 14. 1995.

MacGregor, Arthur. "Bone skates: A review of the evidence." *Archaeological Journal* 133 (1976): 57–74.

Mallet, Paul Henri. *Northern Antiquities: Or a Description of the Manners, Customs, Religion and Laws of the Ancient Danes, Including Those of Our Own Saxon Ancestors*. Translated by Thomas Percy. London: T. Carnan, 1770.

"Monthly catalogue." *The Critical Review: Or, Annals of Literature* 33 (1772): 170–184.

"Monthly catalogue, for May, 1772." *The Monthly Review; or, Literary Journal* 46 (1772): 530–548.

Mulder, Niko. "Patent ontwerp — een vroege klapschaats? (2)." *Kouwe Drukte* 3, no. 7 (December 1999): 5.

———. "Ten IJse (1)." *Kouwe Drukte* 12, no. 33 (October 2008): 25–30.

Musarum Anglicanarum Analecta. Vol. 2. Oxford: J. Crosley, 1699.

New York Public Library. "The Spalding baseball collection." *Bulletin of the New York Public Library* 26, no. 1 (January 1922): 86–127.

Norton, Rictor. "Jones, Captain Robert." In *Who's Who in Gay and Lesbian History: From Antiquity to World War II*, second ed., edited by Robert Aldrich and Gary Wotherspoon, 275. New York: Routledge, 2002.

———. "The first public debate about homosexuality in England: News reports concerning the case of Captain Jones, 1772." In *Homosexuality in Eighteenth-Century England: A Sourcebook*. 2004; updated 8 August 2022.

———. "The first public debate about homosexuality in England: The Case of Captain Jones, 1772." In *The Gay Subculture in Georgian England*. 2004; updated 10 May 2014.

———, ed. "The trial of Robert Jones, 1772." In *Homosexuality in Eighteenth-Century England: A Sourcebook*. 2004.

Percy, Sholto, and Reuben Percy. *The Percy Anecdotes: Anecdotes of Pastime.* London: T. Boys, 1821.

Percy, Thomas, trans. *Five Pieces of Runic Poetry, Translated from the Islandic Language.* London: R. and J. Dodsley, 1763.

Porter, Enid. "Fen Skating." *Folk Life* 7 (1969): 43–59.

Rimbault, Edward F. *Old Ballads Illustrating the Great Frost of 1683–4 and the Fair on the River Thames.* London: T. Richards for the Percy Society, 1844.

Säve, P. A., and H. Gustavson. *Gotländska lekar.* Vol. 1. Svenska lekar. Uppsala: Almqvist och Wichsells Boktryckeri AB, 1948.

Skinner, Stephen. *Etymologicon linguæ Anglicanæ.* London: H. Brome, 1671.

Sloan, Michelle. *The Edinburgh Skating Club.* Edinburgh: Polygon Books, 2022.

Smith, Charles Roach. *Collectanea Antiqua: Etchings and Notices of Ancient Remains Illustrative of the Habits, Customs, and History of Past Ages.* London: J. R. Smith, 1848.

Smith, Charles Roach, and Alfred Smee. "Bone Skate Found at Moorfield." *Archæologia, or Miscellaneous Tracts Relating to Antiquity* 29 (1842): 397–399.

Stephenson, Richard. "In the Beginning." *Skating*, June 1970, 8–9.

Story, G. M. "Cormack, William Eppes (Epps)." In *Dictionary of Canadian Biography*, vol. 9. Toronto: University of Toronto, 2003.

Strutt, Joseph. *Gil-Gamena Angel-deod. Or, the Sports and Pastimes of the People of England*. London: T. Bensley, 1801.

Thomson, Duncan, and Lynne Gladstone-Millar. *The Skating Minister: The Story behind the Painting*. Edinburgh: National Galleries of Scotland, 2004.

Thurber, B. A. *Skates Made of Bone: A History*. Jefferson, NC: McFarland, 2020.

Tytler, James, ed. *Encyclopædia Britannica*. Second ed. Vol. 10. Edinburgh: J. Balfour & Co., et al., 1783.

Vandervell, H. E. *The Figure Skate: A Research into the Form of Blade Best Adapted to Curvilinear Skating*. London: Straker Brothers, 1901.

Vandervell, H. E., and T. Maxwell Witham. *A System of Figure-Skating, Being the Theory and Practice of the Art as Developed in England, with a Glance at Its Origin and History*. London: Macmillan & Company, 1869.

Whyte, James Christie. *History of the British Turf*. London: Henry Colburn, 1840.

Withey, Alun. *Technology, Self-Fashioning and Politeness in Eighteenth-Century Britain*. New York: Palgrave Macmillan, 2016.

Woodcroft, Bennet. *Alphabetical Index of Patentees of Inventions*. First published in 1854. London: Evelyn, Adams, & MacKay, 1969.

Woodward, G. M. *Eccentric Excursions: or, Literary and Pictorial Sketches of Countenance, Character and Country in different parts of England and South Wales*. London: Allen & Co., 1796.

Woudenberg, Sybolt. "Paar van de dominee?" *Kouwe Drukte* 17, no. 49 (December 2013): 6.

Zippel, Otto. "Entstehungs- und Entwicklungsgeschichte von Thomsons «Winter»." PhD diss., Friedrich-Wilhelms-Universität zu Berlin, 1907.

———. *Thomson's Seasons: Critical Edition*. Berlin: Mayer & Müller, 1908.

www.ingramcontent.com/pod-product-compliance
Lightning Source LLC
Chambersburg PA
CBHW070100080526
44586CB00013B/1129